An
EMERGING
INDEPENDENT
AMERICAN
ECONOMY
1815-1875

Edited by
Joseph R. Frese, S.J.
and
Jacob Judd

The Sleepy Hollow Press
and
Rockefeller Archive Center

Library of Congress Cataloging in Publication Data
Main entry under title:
An emerging independent American economy, 1815–1875.
  Includes index.
  1. Business enterprises — United States — History — Addresses,
essays, lectures. 2. United States — Industries — History —
Addresses, essays, lectures.
I. Frese, Joseph R.   II. Judd, Jacob

HF5343.E47   338.0973   80-15195
ISBN O-912882-40-9

First Printing

For information, address the publisher:
The Sleepy Hollow Press
Sleepy Hollow Restorations, Inc.
Tarrytown, New York 10591

ISBN O-912882-40-9
Library of Congress Catalog Card Number 80-15195

Manufactured in the United States of America

Contents

Introduction

This is the second in a series of books on American business. The series evolved from discussions of the historical evolution of American capitalism at the annual Conference on American Economic Enterprise sponsored jointly by the Rockefeller Archive Center and Sleepy Hollow Restorations.

It is no secret that, for some years now, American capitalism has come in for a great deal of criticism. In nineteenth-century America the criticism of the capitalistic system came mostly from the viewpoint of labor—to the effect that labor was not getting its share of the rewards. The criticism was not centered as much on capitalism itself as on the distribution of the profits. Labor wanted more. It was not simply an economic group struggling to survive within a confined class structure; rather, it was the American workingman viewing himself as a capitalist without money. He wanted money not just to improve his lot as a laborer, but as a means by which he could set himself up in business. The laborer envisioned a future as an independent capitalist, not simply as a laborer with money. Thus the capitalistic system—or mind-set—then involved not only the business elite but all Americans.

In the nineteenth century there was little or no attempt in the United States to abolish the capitalistic system. That there were abuses—especially in other countries, such as England—Americans were willing to admit. Yet, while no one wanted to eliminate the system itself, some sought alternative ways of coping with it. The many communal groups founded in the first half of the century were primarily efforts to escape from the inherent evils they associated with the developing society. Rather than the destruction of that society, their objective was the creation of a haven for themselves. Among the mainstream in society, even the laborer wanted to take advantage of the emergent capitalistic system. Indeed, both industrialists and members of the working class—the owner and the laborer alike—wanted the system left in place so that each might use it for his own good. Since the laborer saw capitalism as a means by which he could become a capitalist, he wanted capitalism to remain—cleaned up a bit, perhaps, but not destroyed.

More recently, the criticism of American capitalism has extended beyond the factory and the picket line. It has become the subject of an intellectual critique which wonders if capitalism itself is not substantially evil. Rather than concentrating on abuses of the system, as in the past, it is the system itself which currently is under attack. Is the complex American system, with its multinational conglomerates, its dominance in the third world, its influence in international finance, so internally unjust that it cannot be purified? Does the working of the system necessarily lead to oppression, injustice, and inequity? Are these gross defects remediable? Is American capitalism worth saving—and what are the alternatives?

Marxism always claimed that capitalism was essentially evil. It was not, therefore, in the best interests of their political-economic ideology for true Marxists to be concerned with efforts to reform capitalism. Indeed, since the system is inherently evil in itself, according to their thought, no reform is

iv

possible; capitalism must be destroyed. Lately, such a Marxian ideological-intellectual evaluation — that capitalism is substantially corrupt—has been endorsed by many people.

In recent times an increasing number of scholars—theologians, philosophers, sociologists—decry capitalism as a system. They no longer just complain of the abuses that are inevitable in all systems; rather, recent emphasis is upon complaints of a substantive nature. Among such trends, liberation theology is attempting to find a new social order that is determined neither by modern capitalism nor by Marxism. In addition, philosophers are increasingly concerned with the poor and the oppressed in modern society.[1]

These questions, of course, are currents in the intellectual atmosphere. Yet basic to all such intellectual questioning is a determination as to what "capitalism" or the American system really is. Too few have bothered to define it. What is primarily considered is that something is substantially wrong with the system as it has evolved. Critics are prone to suggest that there is too much poverty, starvation, and oppression in a world which seems to have been created by capitalism.

It is only natural that other questions arise in this atmosphere. How did capitalism really begin in America? How did people make money? How did people get rich? Obviously, in the beginning it was not a question of the system or of international conglomerates. While every man was far from being on an equal footing in the socio-economic structure, he looked upon himself as having the capabilities to improve his status. Here in this nascent country, it was always thought that everyone had a chance to become wealthy—to become a capitalist, that is.

v

In the first volume in this series, Business Enterprise in Early New York, *we sought to focus on how money was made, how people in early America became rich. Ironically, it is apparent that many of the great speculators in government supplies, in banking, and in land actually failed in such ventures. If this was the capitalistic system, it hardly proved to be the road to wealth.*

In this second volume, the concentration is not so much on the individual as on the mechanisms of business. The first half of the nineteenth century in America—the focal point of this study—was a period of great idealism. Having won political independence and expanded into an enormous territory, Americans were zealous to exploit the new-found wealth. Rather than viewing this as exploitation, however, the vast majority considered such resource use and rapid expansion as necessary uses of the God-given abundance found principally on the frontier.

Abundant resources were not an isolated factor in gaining our economic independence. We also had to exploit technology. As Professor Glenn Porter explains in the opening essay, Americans at that time were essentially tinkerers rather than inventors. They were technicians starting with a European background which was exploited in America. The enormous riches of the nation led them to a willingness to discard the old and to begin anew. There was not need for conservation, and the abundance of material possessions led in turn to ever-new advanced technology.

According to Professor Porter, we are increasing our understanding of the significant part technology played in expanding business enterprise. Subsequently, we changed our ideological approach to the study of business, economics, technoloy, and science. Originally, the history of business concentrated on the study of technology; now it has developed into a study of economics. The history of science has now been invaded by the history of technology.

The period was also characterized by individualism. It was the individual who pushed westward, the individual who founded new enterprise, the individual who won a place in society.

While it was an age of new frontiers and individual enthusiasm, it was still an age of old energy. The sources of energy to which we are accustomed and which contribute to so much of our present-day life style were unknown in the first half of the nineteenth century. Professor Dolores Greenberg points out that our extensive use of fossil fuels for energy did not begin until the 1880's. In the period covered by these essays, the reliance was on muscle energy. Perhaps this can be more readily understood when we realize population distribution. America had not yet become a nation of cities. We were essentially a rural population. Hence our energy needs were essentially different. These needs were supplied, not by fossil or mineral fuels, but by draft animals and humans.

This essay by Professor Greenberg, like many in this series, will naturally provoke questions among readers: Is it possible for a nation to become economically independent without the use of fossil fuels? What would happen if a nation suddenly abolished the combustion engine? Would we seek a rural life again and let the cities decay? Would we be able to re-create the same ideals, enthusiasms—and energy—of the first half of the nineteenth century? Or, conversely, did ideals and en-

thusiasm flow from the abundance of fuel available?

The issues of liberty and independence which arise today in relation to government and the control of energy had no place in the first half of the nineteenth century. Today, whoever controls the sources of energy controls business. But in the first half of the nineteenth century, no one could control the sources of energy without controlling people. The one American civilization based on slavery was destroyed. If we discover latent sources of energy in ourselves in the future, as we did in the past, then no one could control business without first destroying individual freedom.

Further questions arise: Can a present-day nation gain economic independence based on a rural economy? Must one be industrialized to be independent? Can an "industrial" society survive without fossil fuels? Are we destined to return in some way to the first half of the nineteenth century?

Once some of the basics of New York business enterprise in the first half of the nineteenth century have been put forth— particularly energy and technology—it is important to study the implementation of the new economic structure. Essential to such development, as Professor John F. Stover explains, were the appearances of turnpikes and canals. Further emphasizing the financial importance of the Northeast, he notes that few of these transportation developments were to be found west of Ohio or south of Virginia.

The turnpikes were the first to appear. While they obviously came into being for the distribution of goods, they were so limited that only goods high in value or low in weight could be economically shipped over them. Although turnpikes were both state and privately financed, few, if any, were profitable.

Their financial problems came, in part, from "shunpikes" purposely created to escape payment of tolls on officially recognized turnpikes. In addition, the turnpikes were not in use long enough to realize their full potential, or their profit. Despite their shortcomings, they did contribute to the growth of America. As a byproduct, improved stage coaches introduced to take advantage of the turnpikes helped satisfy and stimulate the American—and, indeed, the tourist's—appetite for travel. They also helped immeasurably toward national unity.

If turnpikes, in general, were not financially successful, the Erie Canal made all states envious of its rate of return on initial investment. The four-foot-deep ditch proved to be unbelievably lucrative. With a series of locks to control water levels and aqueducts to cross streams, the Erie was successful from the beginning. This was due in part to the speed with which it was constructed. The system of subcontracting to local farmers opened the canal in a rapidly completed series of sections. The whole project caught the tide of history: it was conceived at the proper moment in the right place and completed in time to be successful. Few other canals could match this record. The Pennsylvania Main Line had to contend with too-difficult terrain. Others came into being too late. The railroads, with their speed, their flexibility to circumvent geographical obstacles, and their capability to operate through the winter season, soon won control of the freight business. Only a few coal canals remained financially successful. The others gave way to new modes of transportation, as had the turnpikes before them.

From turnpikes and canals, one must necessarily turn to

railroads. Since our concentration is primarily on New York, it is the New York Central Railroad that becomes the focus of the next two essays. They go beyond being a survey of the structuring of the Central to provide detailed studies of the supply of both iron and money, which were the sinews of that structure. Interestingly, much of these basic necessities came from England.

When the original lines of the New York Central were under construction, not one foundry in the United States existed capable of rolling iron rail. Until this deficit could be remedied, all rail had to be purchased abroad. Great Britain, principally South Wales, became the chief supplier of rails for the Central. The consequence was an enormous trade in custom-made rails and in chartered ships, and a reliance on scheduled sailings and a confronting of the hazards of oceanic travel in all weather.

Agents soon abounded as suppliers to various sections of the future New York Central system. No agent was more successful in combining activities related to railroad construction than Erastus Corning, the central figure in Ann M. Scanlon's study. Corning purchased a hardware business, an iron foundry and furnace, an iron mill—which grew, under his tutelage, into one of the largest iron and steel firms in the United States. Furthermore, seeing the interrelations of iron and the railroads, he soon began purchasing railroad stock. Commencing with investment as early as 1831 in the Mohawk and Hudson, he expanded his holdings until he had acquired stock in virtually every railroad in central and western New York.

Finally, Corning became an iron agent, purchasing railroad iron for the developing companies of New York. With extensive credit from the Barings in London, he increasingly widened his activities. At the same time, he became more active in railroad management, becoming in time the president of the New York Central. His multiple activities came under scrutiny by a committee of inquiry which cleared Corning of any wrongdoing, but it was clear that his presidency of the railroad had not harmed his profits as a manufacturer and as a purchasing agent. While Corning did not hold a monopoly, he still did well from his positions. Yet most of these purchases were made in Great Britain, and that nation long remained the chief supplier of rails to the Central.

Professor Harry H. Pierce adds to the story of the New York Central with an in-depth study of the shareholders of the railroad. From his detailed research in original sources, Professor Pierce points out that, unlike other American railroads, the Central sold no securities for rails. Indeed, no foreign capital was invested in the early components of the Central system in any significant amount until after the consolidation of 1853. Furthermore, it was not until the late-nineteenth-century development of limited liability that people of more moderate means in England were encouraged to enter the market. The first investors were generally the rich merchants, bankers, brokers, and civil servants who alone had risk capital. Many of these shares were later re-sold by the English at the time of the Civil War.

According to Professor Pierce, the one great event which opened the New York Central to widespread—even English—investment was the decision of William H. Vanderbilt to sell 350,000 shares through the Jay Gould syndicate. This enormous offering enabled Vanderbilt to re-invest his wealth, the

English to buy into the Central, and Jay Gould to realize almost $1,000,000 from the transaction. As a result, English shareholders increased in number from 308 in 1875 to 3,224 in 1885. This time it was the ordinary Englishman who made the investment. The New World since its discovery has always been looked upon as a place for venturesome capital.

In Professor Edward Pessen's discussion of the business elite in New York, he develops the point that the business leaders were not manufacturers or industrialists but merchants with fingers in many pies. Their wealth came from diversified sources—and almost always included some banking interests.

Such diversification enabled the New York merchant to recover more easily from economic panics and depressions. It provided economic stability and continuity as the merchants quickly rebuilt lost fortunes. Above all, it gave the merchants—the elite of urban society—a control over that society. With power over property, banks, real estate, and industrial production, the merchants established economic policies and controlled the politics which protected them. Successful businessmen saw to the passage of laws that helped the propertied classes. Yet the elite were not any more selfish than other classes. Indeed, they were public-spirited, for to be public-spirited required both wealth and protection. It was a comforting social doctrine, and a capitalistic mind-set was well on its way toward development.

Where Professor Pessen emphasizes the rise of the business elite in New York, Professor Robert Lekachman highlights the decline of the entrepreneur. In the nineteenth century the business tycoon or robber baron was individualistic and suffered no agonies of conscience in his struggle to dominate or rule an industry. These men controlled the legislature just as Professor Pessen's elite saw to the passage of favorable laws. They succeeded because other institutions were weak and proved to be hardly a worthy opposition. Antitrust legislation and court suits were tolerated as long as they did not interfere with business. The businessman was a model to be followed or a winner to be admired. His achievement appealed to something in all men—which is, perhaps, why the game of Monopoly has remained so popular.

Yet there came a change. The corporate leaders declined. Conservative unions talked of possible government control of utilities. Business still had power over taxes, trade policy, and labor laws, but the corporate leader was no longer admired— or even known. Real income and financial mobility increased for all. Industry became bureaucratic and concerned with material wealth. It had lost its romance and legend.

Business—and America—now faces the uncertain future. It is really a future of reparations, where damage to the fabric must be repaired. The cleanup of polluted areas and the sheer maintenance of the physical structure are going to require an enormous amount of the money available. What is to happen when we come to a no-growth economy? It will mean controversy on taxes and federal grants, which will lead to a policy struggle between free enterprise and the new breed of planners. Somehow there must be a national policy for social stability. Out of it will come a different America.

Joseph R. Frese, S.J.
Cornwall, New York

Jacob Judd
Tarrytown, New York

Note

1. For a discussion of liberation theology, see, Robert M. Brown, *Theology in a New Key: Responding to Liberation Themes* (Philadelphia, 1978) ; José M. Bonino, *Christians and Marxists* (Grand Rapids, Mich., 1976) ; Enrique D. Dussel, *History and the Theology of Liberation: A Latin American Perspective* (Maryknoll, N.Y., 1976).

    Recent writings in business ethics include, Donald G. Jones, *A Bibliography of Business Ethics, 1971–1975* (Charlottesville, Va., 1977) ; *Business and Professional Ethics: A Quarterly Newsletter* (Troy, N.Y.) ; Tom L. Beauchamp and Norman Bowie, eds., *Ethical Theory and Business* (Englewood Cliffs, N.J., 1979).

    Sociologists and political theorists have voluminously studied the question. Among some recent works are, Henry Fairlie, *The Spoiled Child of the Western World: The Miscarriage of the American Idea in Our Time* (New York, 1976) ; Daniel Bell and Irving Kristol, eds., *Capitalism Today* (New York, 1971) ; E. F. Schumacher, *Small is Beautiful* (New York, 1977) ; Mary G. Powers and Joan J. Holmberg, "Occupational Status Scores: Changes Introduced By The Inclusion of Women," *Demography*, XV:2 (May, 1978) ; Michael Harrington, *The Twilight of Capitalism* (New York, 1976).

Technology and Business in the American Economy

Glenn Porter

The process of the creation and diffusion of new technologies has always been at the heart of changes in the American economy.[1] Within the fundamental context set by the attitudes and values of the American people on the one hand and our particular mix of what economists call "factor endowments" on the other, the pace and pattern of the spread of new technologies have done much to define our economic past. Furthermore, the diffusion of new productive devices, processes, and modes of organization has always occurred primarily within the business system, within the "private" sector of American economic enterprise. As a result, there has been a peculiar and an extremely strong link between American business and American technology throughout the course of our history. Within the last two decades, there has also come to be a similar link between these two academic subdisciplines, business history and the history of technology. This essay, then, concerns itself with both the history—what happened in the past —and with the historiography of technology and business.

American Business and Technology since 1815

By far the greatest single difference between the nineteenth
and the twentieth century in American economic history is the
relative importance of government in the economy in the two
periods. A significant dimension of that difference is the fact
that government played a far smaller role in encouraging and
influencing the creation and diffusion of new technologies in
the last century than in the present one. Throughout our economic past—but particularly in the era in which we were
engaged in establishing an independent economy—technical
change has always made its impact primarily within the setting of the private firm. If we wish, therefore, to understand
the root causes of technical changes, their sources, and the
mechanisms by which they arose and spread, it is within the
business system that we must mainly look. Government did, of
course, play a noteworthy part—by establishing and enforcing
stability and the fundamental "rules of the game" politically and economically, by effecting the systems of patents
and tariffs, by making available selective bounties and quasi-
monopolies, by subsidizing certain very important sectors
(such as arms manufacture), and in other ways.[2] The ability
of the political system to influence technical changes, however,
was always limited by the market. Because of that, this paper
focuses on the business setting.

It also seeks to approach the problem of the origin and
diffusion of technical change in a relatively abstract manner.
That is, I wish to offer some tentative generalizations about
the processes and mechanisms of such change over time in the
case of the United States, particularly within the manufactur-

ing sector. It will be difficult for historians of technology and of business to deal more satisfactorily with this topic unless they employ both a comparative approach and a set of organizing hypotheses. The first proposition, of course, is that the most fruitful territory lies at the nexus of business and technology.

A second proposition is, to some extent, antithetical to the "independent economy" theme of this book, because it posits that technical change in America owed a very great debt to European antecedents. Despite the "ingenious Yankee" stereotype, it seems likely that the majority of advances in technology in the United States in the nineteenth century had European origins. There were, to be sure, a number of important exceptions. Because of the enormously greater availability of some raw materials in the American economy—particularly wood and leather — Americans proved very adept at technical advances associated with the use of those materials. Similarly, the central economic role of the production of grains and breadstuffs in the United States made it understandable that American milling technology led the world in the early stages of the Industrial Revolution. And, for reasons still vigorously debated, there had come to exist in many industries by the time of the Crystal Palace Exhibition in London in 1851 a complicated set of interrelated technical and economic arrangements that eventually came to be known by the shorthand phrase, "the American system of manufactures."[3] Despite these and a number of other examples of Yankee ingenuity, the *general* technical superiority of nineteenth-century Europe—and particularly of the United Kingdom— seems beyond reasonable doubt. The implications of this

pattern of non-American origins for most technical changes
in the nineteenth-century United States is clear: we must pay
much more attention than we have in the past to European
developments, and to the process of the transatlantic diffusion
of new ways of doing things. Business historians are probably
guilty of more instances of this sort of provincialism than are
historians of technology, but there is bounteous room for improvement all around on this score.

And what is it, exactly, that needs to be better understood?
First, we need to know more about the causes of technical
change. In this connection I might observe, as an aside, that it
may well prove more fruitful to focus greater energy on the
problem of the adoption of new forms of technics than on their
creation. The question of how invention occurs, of how a new
device or process or set of arrangements comes into existence,
has always been vital, if not paramount, in the history of
technology. This focus on invention, while perfectly understandable and productive, has also had its negative aspects.
It has, for example, often buttressed the simplistic "great
man" view of technical change. And, because it is virtually
impossible to answer such questions as "who invented the
steam engine," approaching change via a focus on invention
sometimes leads to pointless definitional hairsplitting and a
stultifying consideration of "firsts" in the history of technics.
Even worse, because the process of creation often is explic-
able only through reference to a set of unique circumstances,
accidents, or personality quirks in the inventor, the emphasis
on invention often serves to reinforce a historical mind-set
that tends to view events as unique, disassociated occurrences
and sees the world as chaotic and non-rational. By switching

the arena for investigation from that of invention to innovation, many of these problems can be overcome. We should perhaps try to refrain from asking how mankind created all the things ever invented, and instead ask: Of all those things, why did certain ones have greater impact than others in given times and places? This will aid in the identification of patterns and will also compel us to consider technical change in its wider social, political, and economic contexts, since it is only within those contexts that we can understand why one thing had more impact than another. If our main concern should lie with innovation, then, what is it that we need to know about the causes of technical change?

For the United States, we need to know to what extent the story of that change can be accounted for by reference to economic explanations, and to what extent it cannot. It seems safe to say that the most common major explanations of the spread of new technologies lie in this realm; the desirability of reducing labor costs, of using less raw materials, of substituting cheaper for dearer raw materials, of increasing profits or strengthening a firm's market position by introducing or by suppressing a new product or process are all familiar examples of categories of economic explanations of technical change in history. The use of economic theory to elucidate technical change has yielded some excellent results, particularly in the work of Nathan Rosenberg.[4] For a complex set of reasons that I will consider later, however, neither historians of technology nor business historians have found neoclassical economics and its subdiscipline, microeconomics, very satisfying as a methodology. Recognizing the explanatory power of material self-interest in the American culture has not meant recognizing any strong utility for economics as a guide for those trained as historians.

This is true in part because of the widespread perception that motivations other than material self-interest have also guided the behavior of persons in the past. These include, pre-eminently, the manifold but closely related forms of non-material self-interest, such as the search for power and dominance over others, and the desire to achieve fame.[5] But they have also included some considerations rather far removed from that realm, such as a desire for greater technical perfection or greater technical sophistication for its own sake, quite apart from the question of whether the new technologies will yield some economic advantage. This particular source of technical change, the search for a more satisfying or somehow inherently more technically appealing contrivance or arrangement, appears to have been an important part of what is sometimes termed "the engineering mind." It lies near the center of the technical specialist's fascination with such concepts as the relative efficiency of various engines or turbines, which are deemed of interest wholly aside from any questions of relative cost. Along with other factors, it also helps to explain why some clear national differences emerged in technological styles, such as the contrast in the nineteenth century between the French taste for elegant, costly, mathematically satisfying civil engineering systems and the Americans' much less elegant, rough-and-ready approach, in which business considerations played a relatively larger part.[6] Though it is often alloyed with such urgings as the wish to be "up to date" or to demonstrate some presumed national, ethnic, or other form of group superiority, the need to achieve purely technical improvement or sophistication is evident.

Another sort of motivation should be mentioned here, one that I have seen emphasized by both historians of technology and anthropologists. That is simply the motivation of play. Although its role in invention is probably greater than in innovation, the simple self-amusement of the human mind and our capacity for wonder are clearly factors that should not be ignored in any effort to understand technical change in the past. Indeed, anthropologists who study rigidly traditional cultures that normally undergo change only very slowly argue that play can be virtually the only avenue for the introduction of change in such societies. Even in our own culture it is present in the bundle of motives with which we effect new technologies; anyone who watched the engineer-astronauts romping on the surface of the moon or in the zero gravity of space flight can readily imagine the whole space program as an overblown adult toy.

In addition to refining our notions of the root motivations for the adoption of new technics, we need to identify the categories of mechanisms for change and to try to assess their relative importance over time. There is, for example, a fairly well articulated view that in developing societies, such as the early-nineteenth-century United States, the introduction and spread of new technologies often depended on the physical transfer of the skilled men and the machines that embodied those novel technologies. Because the recipient culture or firm lacked a reservoir of people knowledgeable about the new devices or processes, it was often necessary to import the machines or the people who had actually operated them. Presumably, it was in recognition of this means of technical transfer that so many political units sought to interfere with the flow of the inventors, skilléd mechanics, and new productive devices. For example, the futile efforts of the British government to stop the "leakage" of the technology of the Industrial Revolution are well documented,[7] and state governments in the United States tried the same thing, with equally poor results.[8]

The importance of knowledgeable individuals and of the machines themselves in spreading new technologies in the early stages of economic development is related to the phenomenon known as "non-verbal technology."[9] That phrase refers to situations in which some critical elements in the efficient operation of a new technology resist reduction to written form, and can only be acquired through actual experience with the novel processes or devices. It was possible, for example, for Americans to read descriptions and observe drawings of British textile technology, but quite another matter to create and efficiently operate similar textile factories without either the help of experienced Britons or the importation of textile machinery. Over time, as the general process of socio-economic development proceeded, the importance of non-verbal technology and of the men-and-machines mechanism for transfer declined, though it never disappeared entirely. As a less developed culture, region, or firm came to have a larger domestic reservoir of knowledge and talent, not only in the form of men and machines but also in the form of permanent institutions such as universities, technical societies, and technical institutes, it became increasingly easy for new technics to be adopted once they had appeared in the "outside world."

Obviously, in order for those new and presumably better

mousetraps to spread, it was necessary that good channels of communication be open between the people who had and those who did not have the devices in question. In the early stages of development, those channels were often informal, and much depended on personal contacts among networks of manufacturers and technical people.[10] Correspondence and personal visits, both within the United States and across the Atlantic, were probably the major communications mechanisms in the early period. Furthermore, there is much evidence of a widespread openness to such fact-finding travels, despite all that we might expect to find in the way of industrial secrecy.[11] Again, the relative importance of personal contacts and of travels to others' manufactories very likely shrank with the expansion of more formal and more "standardized" methods of communication.

The earliest form of those more generally available methods in the United States, of course, was printed descriptions, plans, and "recipes" for new technics. The role of printed materials in the spread of new technologies grew over time, and surely was less in the early nineteenth century than later. Evald Rink's thorough bibliography of technical Americana before the year 1831 demonstrates the progressive and explosive growth in printed matter relating to technology in the closing decades of the eighteenth century and the opening ones of the nineteenth.[12] The tendency toward the increasing importance over time of formal and impersonal mechanisms for the spread of new technologies is clearly a central theme in the history of American technology and business.

Thus far we have considered very abstract notions, and it would perhaps be useful to shift the focus for a time down to the level of the individual firm. By what kinds of mechanisms did new devices or procedures come to be adopted by the American manufacturer? Many, indeed probably most, of them came to his attention from the "outside," rather than being internally generated within the firm. A surprising proportion of those came *unbidden* to him. That is, the world beyond his factory generated and offered to him a vast array of alleged improvements, which he often learned about without having actively sought them. Initially, letters and visits came from persons who had invented (or claimed to have invented) some new peruna; later these elixirs (some of which were even genuine advances) were advertised. If the new technique seemed sufficiently promising, or if the problem it was said to resolve seemed sufficiently pressing, he would investigate this opportunity offered him by his environment.[13] More often, perhaps, the manufacturer engaged in what is called in economic jargon "search activities": he actively sought out information about new things and access to them. At first he would visit similar manufactories at home or abroad, or he would write to the knowledgeable people he knew. He might well seek to entice the needed skilled and experienced workmen to his employ, or try to buy or lease the new devices. More and more as time passed he could turn to publications, to technical institutions, to firms with general skills in solving technical problems (such as those in the machine tool industry), to universities, and to government for assistance.

In addition to the pattern of the appearance of new things in the world outside the manufacturing firm, there was the internal mechanism for their generation. In general, this phenomenon has been less well studied than that of the "outside" appearance. And, to the extent that it has been studied, there has been much more focus on the invention of the spectacular, major technologies than on the cumulative, smaller advances. The careful study of this less glamorous but nonetheless very significant process of change via activities inside the firm itself will yield important insights. It should prove especially helpful in refining our understanding of the root motivations for the generation of technical change.

Within the context of internally generated change, some observations can be made about change over time. In the early period, the economic landscape was peopled with small firms and with generalists. This meant that anyone concerned with technical matters within the firm was also usually concerned with management. It also meant that antebellum manufacturers thought it perfectly natural for them to deal with several kinds of widely separated technologies. A producer of iron, for example, might well experiment not only with the techniques of iron production, but with such others as the generation and transmission of power or even with improvements in the transportation of his raw materials or finished goods. As the size of the firm grew, and as more and more outside expertise for those ancillary technologies could be brought or hired over time, specialization grew. Firms tended to focus their energies on improving their major technology, and, if the demand was great enough and the firm large enough, technical problems became the province of full-time specialists rather than part-time generalists. In the large firms in science-based industries, especially in electrical manufactures, chemical production, communications, and pharmaceuticals, the trend toward specialization eventually produced modern research and development departments inside business. The importance of formal educational training for technical specialists also increased as the nineteenth century progressed, and such educational institutions as Worcester Polytechnic, Rensselaer Polytechnic, and the Massachusetts Institute of Technology became vital training centers for managers and engineers.[14]

Finally, another major trend became apparent—the relentless tendency for policy questions concerning business and technology to be resolved at least partially within the political arena rather than inside the "private" sector. As government's share of national income grew, and as more and more public scrutiny was turned on the process by which industrialists and engineers made decisions that shaped Americans' daily lives, the evolution of technical change became ever more explicitly tied to the political process and the distribution of power in American society. Although this phenomenon is pre-eminently characteristic of the modern world of business and technology in the United States, it was present from the beginnings and it grew more significant over time as Americans built their technical civilization from its late-eighteenth-century foundations. The significance of that particular trend will lead future study in the history of technology and industry inevitably toward more attention to the social and political context of technical change.

Having considered some of the major questions that need to be explored in the terrain where business and technology overlap in the history of the American economy, and having reviewed some of the trends over time on that terrain, it is appropriate also to examine the recent evolution of the two academic subdisciplines, the history of technology and business history. This can permit us to see whether historians are moving in a direction that may yield good results relatively soon. I believe that they have indeed been so moving, though they had done so largely unconsciously until very recently.

The Historiography of Technology and Business

Every American historian soon learns that he can apparently add authority and wisdom to his lectures, essays, and books by larding them with quotations from Alexis de Tocqueville's great classic, *Democracy in America*. So many-sided and profound is Tocqueville's book that something from it can be found that suits any occasion. In the history of technology there is a similar source: Lewis Mumford's *Technics and Civilization*, first published in 1934. Any commentary on technology and business should consult the father of the history of technology and his master work. There we find that "although capitalism and technics must be clearly distinguished at every stage, one conditioned the other and reacted upon it. . . . Whether machines would have been invented so rapidly and pushed so zealously without the extra incentive of commercial profit is extremely doubtful. . . . [There was a] close historical association" between "modern technics and modern capitalism . . . the style of the machine has been powerfully influenced by capitalism." [15]

Nor did the influence flow in one direction only. The evolution of business has been powerfully shaped by technical change, particularly by the advancing technologies for transportation, communication, and the generation and transmission of power. One could look to many sources to confirm the fact that technology has profoundly altered business. One of the most dramatic recent confirmations was that offered in the work of a leading and highly influential historian of American business, Harvard University's Alfred D. Chandler, Jr. Consider his 1977 book, *The Visible Hand: The Managerial Revolution in American Business*, which won both the Bancroft and Pulitzer prizes in history. One could reasonably infer from Chandler's work that nothing has so influenced the structure and behavior of the modern corporation and of the whole of modern industry as has technology. Indeed, it is arguable that his explanation of the history of business in the United States in the last century and a half verges on technological determinism. A few sentences from the summary chapter of *The Visible Hand* will perhaps illustrate the point. "In production," Chandler writes, "the first modern managers came in those industries and enterprises where technology permitted several processes of production to be carried on within a single factory or works." "Technological innovation, the rapid growth and spread of population, and expanding per capita income made the processes of production and distribution more complex and increased the speed and volume of the flow of materials through them. . . . As technology became both more complex and more productive, and as markets continued to expand, . . . managers assumed command in the central sectors of the American economy."[16]

Indeed, in growing recognition of extensive shared interests, I believe that there has been in the last two decades a drawing together of the two fields, the history of business and that of technology. Scholars in both areas have moved away from an intellectual association with what had earlier seemed a closely related discipline. In the case of business history, the movement has been away from economic history, and in the case of the history of technology, from the history of science. In the process, there has emerged the beginnings of what promises to be a most fruitful process of intellectual intercourse.

How did this come to be? Perhaps a more logical question would be: Why has it taken so long for it to come to be? These two fields have, as I have already argued, much in common, including the fact that both are clearly central to American history and equally clearly not central to the general American historian's version of the country's past. Indeed, much of what seems distinctive about the history of this nation has to do with technology and business. Other peoples certainly have a more distinguished history of high culture (art, music, literature), and others have a more varied and intricate political past. Several others have even had higher rates of economic growth. But who would seriously argue that any other people have elevated the works of the businessman, the inventor, and the engineer to the high forms and the high places they have achieved in American culture? Those who study the history of business and technology share the feeling that their subjects have been sadly overlooked and undervalued in a profession that has traditionally cared most about Presidents, wars, and diplomacy.

They have also shared, it should be noted, a strong suspicion of theory in history and even, to some extent, a suspicion of generalizations and syntheses in history. Many pioneering

scholars in both areas of study began with a heavy reliance on
the case study and a naive conviction that as soon as a "critical
mass" of isolated case studies was assembled, unifying and
organizing ideas would then emerge.[17] Though much progress
has been made by leading scholars, both fields are to a degree
still struggling to go beyond the isolated case study stage without going so far as to surrender all to the purveyors of theory.

The history of technology has for a long while been linked
to the history of science. For example, the ethical concerns
over "values" in the last few years have generated a mass of
programs in "science, technology, and society" (or "values")
though none, to my knowledge, under the more logical rubric
of "business, technology, and society."[18] In my view, the
alliance between the history of science and the history of technology is an uneasy one, and it has been so for some time.
Historians of science have often looked down on historians of
technology as mere "nuts and bolts" devotees, as relatives
perhaps, but as slightly (and embarrassingly) retarded ones.
The history of science has generally been practiced as a rari-
fied form of intellectual history, an activity often quite different in method and content from the history of technology,
though many important contributions to the history of technology have come from historians of science.[19] For years, the
history of science was the more glamorous and more marketable specialty; historians of technology trailed along on the
periphery. In recent years that situation has changed as the
primitives have waxed while the history of science has waned.
Academic jobs have become relatively plentiful in the history
of technology, and some historians of science now try to
"pass" as specialists in technological history. In 1978, in an-

other sign of the times, the History of Science Society awarded its Pfizer Prize to a work in the history of technology, a book that has, as far as anyone can tell, no history of science in it whatever: Merritt Roe Smith's superb study, *Harper's Ferry Armory and the New Technology*.[20] Some in the history of science who had previously gone to pains to distinguish the differences between their own elevated calling and the history of technology are now engaged in an effort to blur or erase those same distinctions.

As for business historians, their betters have been the practitioners of economic history. The study of business history in America has been a small but distinct subdiscipline ever since the 1920's.[21] The field existed in comparative harmony with the larger area of study of which it was thought a part — economic history — until the events of the last two decades brought the triumph of the "new" economic history. Gradually in the late 1950's and then with a rush in the 1960's, economists replaced historians at the heart of the field of economic history. Insisting on the use of neoclassical economic theory, on careful and explicit specifications of problems, on the use of verifiable hypotheses, and on the primacy of quantitative methods, the "new" economic historians swept the field. They set out to solve their great riddle, the question of how and why sustained, modern economic growth occurred. They would replace the historian's array of inexact methods and vague questions with the more exact one drawn from the "science" of economics. Within a startlingly short time they made a revolution. The major scholarly organization in the field, the Economic History Association, and its organ *The Journal of Economic History*, fell almost entirely to their assault.

The triumph of the "cliometricians" was, in most respects, well deserved. They expanded our knowledge of the American economic past in countless ways, and they led the way in the most elegant and impressive extensions of social science methodologies into the study of history. Unfortunately, their virtually total success and the intellectual intolerance and arrogance that all too often accompanied it, brought some unintended consequences. One such consequence was a striking example of voting with one's feet, in the manner if not on the scale of the Russian army in the First World War after the Russian Revolution; namely, historians (including business historians) exited by the hundreds from the Economic History Association.[22] Another related result is that historians increasingly tend to ignore what they view as the narrow, unintelligible, and slightly silly articles that sometimes appear in *The Journal of Economic History*.

The gulf between business and the now dominant form of economic history is wide and deep. There is little reason to think that that will change soon. As I argued earlier, economics does have some genuinely useful tools and perspectives for the historian of business and technology. On the whole, however, it is a set of ideas that conceptualizes and predicts a static world much more ably than a dynamic, changing one. It posits a unicausal view of change in the economic past, and it requires countless assumptions that are known to be fanciful. It is also a discipline that emphasizes aggregates and overall trends, that takes no interest in the particular or the individual. For those reasons, it has not been a discipline that most trained as historians find congenial or very helpful. There is a greater potential than actual use of economic theory in history, but it is not the panacea its proponents once imagined it to be.

In their drift from economic history on the one hand and the history of science on the other, then, business historians and historians of technology have found increasingly common ground, for the reasons already discussed in this essay. The signs of this development are visible on many fronts. There is, for example, a substantial shared readership and an extensive common ground of intellectual interests between the respective scholarly journals, *Technology and Culture* and *Business History Review*. Historians of technology and business historians often appear on the programs of institutions that shelter those with these same shared interests, such as the Society for the History of Technology, the Business History Conference and its West Coast counterpart the Economic and Business Historical Society, and the Society for Industrial Archeology. In addition, the work of the Historic American Engineering Record reflects an interest in both business history and the history of technology. So do the major academic programs that train young historians to work in this shared field, such as the Hagley Graduate Program at the University of Delaware.

There is emerging a varied network of institutions that nurture study in the still only dimly perceived terrain where the two fields meet. These include not only American universities such as Delaware, Georgia Tech, M.I.T., Rutgers, the University of Pennsylvania, and Johns Hopkins, but also a number of what are now referred to as "public history" institutions.[23] Examples include museums (such as the National Museum of History and Technology at the Smithsonian, the

Hagley Museum, Old Sturbridge Village, Sleepy Hollow Restorations, the Merrimack Valley Textile Museum, and many others), as well as research libraries and archives (such as the Rockefeller Archive Center, the Eleutherian Mills Historical Library, the Bancroft Library, and Baker Library at the Harvard Business School).

Indications of this common ground are also clear in the major bibliographies for the two fields. Henrietta Larson's thorough and superbly annotated *Guide to Business History* (1954), for example, contains many references to sources useful to historians of technology. Conversely, Eugene S. Ferguson's magisterial *Bibliography of the History of Technology* (1968) is an indispensable tool for those interested in business history. Robert W. Lovett's *American Economic and Business History: Information Sources* (1971) contains a major section on the history of science and technology. In the same vein, Evald Rink's massive and as yet unpublished compendium entitled "Technical Americana: A Checklist of Technical Publications Printed before 1831" will prove to be an invaluable guide for scholars in a number of fields, but particularly for historians of technology and of business in the late eighteenth and early nineteenth centuries.

The surest proof, however, of the fact that there is indeed emerging an important and extensive intellectual community of interest lies in recent scholarship. The work of Alfred Chandler has already been mentioned, and he is a key figure in this process. His influence is apparent in many of the major works in the history of technology in the last decade. For example, the *magnum opus* (at least to date) of one of the leading scholars in that area, Thomas P. Hughes' *Elmer Sperry*,

Inventor and Engineer (1971), was done at Johns Hopkins, partly under the aegis of Chandler's Center for the Study of Recent American History.[24] Reese Jenkins' *Images and Enterprise: Technology and the American Photographic Industry, 1839 to 1925* (1975) is another outstanding work that blends business and technology. It is perhaps no accident that Jenkins spent a year with the business history group at Harvard as the Newcomen Postdoctoral Fellow in Business History. Another case in point is Merritt Roe Smith's 1977 book (already mentioned) on Harper's Ferry; Smith has often acknowledged Chandler's influence, and Smith was another in the series of Newcomen Fellows at the Harvard Business School. David A. Hounshell's pathbreaking doctoral dissertation, "From the American System of Manufactures to Mass Production," is yet another impressive example of the powerful results that are flowing from historical analysis that considers both business and technology.[25] Hughes, Jenkins, Smith, and Hounshell have within the last decade all assumed positions of leadership in the history of technology, at the University of Pennsylvania, Rutgers, M.I.T., and the University of Delaware, respectively. On the business history side, there is substantial consideration of the role of technology in the work of many of Chandler's students, such as Harold Livesay, Mary Yeager, Charles Cheape—and Glenn Porter. The same can be said of some of the work of Chandler's successor at Johns Hopkins, Louis Galambos, and of the research of some of those who have worked with Galambos, including Leonard Reich, Joseph Pratt, and Terry Rockefeller.

Two recent contributions to scholarship in particular have underscored the close historical ties between the business and

technical communities, especially in the last century. These
are Edwin T. Layton's *Revolt of the Engineers: Social Responsibility and the American Engineering Profession* (1971),
and David Noble's *America by Design: Science, Technology,
and the Rise of Corporate Capitalism* (1977). Both studies
emphasize the tendency for the practitioners of business and
technology—primarily the industrialist and the engineer—to
come to share the same world-view. Layton's first chapter is
entitled "The Engineer and Business," and he begins it by
declaring that "The engineer is both a scientist and a businessman. Engineering is a scientific profession, yet the test of the
engineer's work lies not in the laboratory, but in the market-
place." Noble argues that the modern corporation, by monop-
olizing research and development and by shaping engineering
education to meet its own needs, has made business and technology virtually one. "Modern technology," he concludes,
"became . . . the racing heart of corporate capitalism." These
studies and numerous others clearly indicate that the scholarly and historical ties between business history and the history of technology are strong and growing stronger.

When, in 1963, Lewis Mumford wrote an introduction for
a reissue of his *Technics and Civilization,* he congratulated
himself warmly for a great many achievements in the book.
Among the most significant of these, in Mumford's admittedly
immodest self-assessment, was the fact that *Technics and
Civilization* "revealed the constant interplay between the
social milieu . . . and the more specific achievements of the
inventor, the industrialist, and the engineer."[26] Intellectual
and institutional forces have been gathering in the last two

decades that offer reason to believe that our collective compre-
hension of the history of technology and industry in American
society is in the process of significant expansion. There is
under way the emergence of what one inclined toward promotion might call the "new industrial history." It lies at the junc-
ture of two unusually important aspects of our past, the history of technology and of business in America, and its task is
to continue the revelation of that "constant interplay between
the social milieu" and "the inventor, the industrialist, and
the engineer."

1. My views on this subject have been shaped by discussions with various friends, colleagues, and students in recent years, particularly those with Merritt Roe Smith, James P. Baughman, Eugene S. Ferguson, John Beer, George Basalla, David Hounshell, William Mulligan, Thomas Bowden, and the participants in the History of Technology (HOT) Lunch group at the University of Delaware. They are not, of course, responsible for any errors, heresies, or apostasies in this paper.

2. Government's influence, as noted above, his grown much stronger in the recent past.

3. See Nathan Rosenberg, ed., *The American System of Manufactures* (Edinburgh, 1969).

4. See, for example, his *Technology and American Economic Growth* (New York, 1972).

5. On the last point, see David A. Hounshell, "The Inventor as Hero in American History," a paper presented at the October, 1979, meeting of the Society for the History of Technology, in Newark, New Jersey.

6. James Edmonson's dissertation, in progress at the University of Delaware, addresses this topic. See also his paper, "The Professionalization of Enginering in 18th and 19th Century France," delivered at the October, 1979, meeting of the Society for the History of Technology.

7. David Jeremy has done particularly good work on these themes in recent years. See his articles, "British Textile Technology Transmission to the United States: The Philadelphia Region Experience, 1770–1820," *Business History Review* (Spring, 1973), 24–25; and "Damming the Flood: British Government Efforts to Check the Outflow of Technicians and Machinery, 1780–1843," *Business History Review* (Spring, 1977), 1–34. See also Chapter VI ("The International Exchange of Men and Machines, 1750–1800") in, A.E. Musson and Eric Robinson, *Science and Technology in the Industrial Revolution* (Manchester, 1969).

8. For example, Thomas Bowden points out that in 1811 "the Delaware legislature made it illegal to encourage artisans to leave the state for employment in similar work beyond its borders." Un-

published paper on "The Traditional Method of Managing Technical Innovation: Black Powder, 1802–1902," 5; copy in the author's possession.

9. I do not know the origin of the term. I first heard it some years ago from Brooke Hindle in a faculty seminar he taught at the Massachusetts Institute of Technology.

10. Anthony F.C. Wallace of the University of Pennsylvania emphasizes this theme, as does John Lozier of Bethany College. Some of the networks are described in Wallace's *Rockdale: The Growth of an American Village in the Early Industrial Revolution* (New York, 1978), and in Lozier's doctoral dissertation, "Taunton and Mason: Cotton Machinery and Locomotive Manufacture in Taunton, Massachusetts, 1811–1861" (Ohio State University, 1978).

11. This was true even in what might seem the most secrecy-prone of industries, arms manufacture. Richard Dwight Glasgow's Ph.D. dissertation, "Prelude to a Naval Renaissance: Ordnance Innovation in the United States Navy during the 1870s" (University of Delaware, 1978), refers to numerous such instances. See also Darwin Stapleton's Ph.D. dissertation, "The Transfer of Technology to the United States in the Nineteenth Century" (University of Delaware, 1975), which documents many examples of information-gathering abroad by persons involved in the American gunpowder, railroading, and iron manufacturing industries.

12. Rink, "Technical Americana: A Checklist of Technical Publications Printed before 1831." This bibliography is at present available only from its author, who is head of the imprints department at the Eleutherian Mills Historical Library, Greenville, Delaware.

13. Many of my views on this process and on the entire phenomenon of technical change in the era of the small firm have been shaped by Thomas Bowden's unpublished essays on the nineteenth-century explosives industry in America: "The Traditional Method of Managing Technical Innovation: Black Powder, 1802–1902," and "Breakdown of the Traditional Approach: Dynamite and Smokeless Powder, 1867–1903."

14. Two of the important studies of this topic are Edwin Layton's *Revolt of the Engineers: Social Responsibility and the American Engineering Profession* (Cleveland, 1971), and David Noble's

America by Design: Science, Technology, and the Rise of Corporate Capitalism (New York, 1977).

15. Mumford, *Technics and Civilization* (New York, 1934, paperback edition 1963), 26–28.

16. Chandler, *The Visible Hand*, 486, 484. The dramatic shift in Chandler's views on the importance of technology in the history of American business can be seen by comparing his classic 1959 essay, "The Beginnings of 'Big Business' in American Industry," *Business History Review* (Spring, 1959), 1–31, with his 1969 article in the Autumn, 1969, issue of the same journal, "The Structure of American Industry in the Twentieth Century: A Historical Overview," 255–98.

17. The business historian who sought from the first (and most successfully) to see business history in its social context rather than in a case study mold, of course, is Thomas Cochran. Almost all of his work points in this direction, but perhaps his *Business in American Life: A History* (New York, 1972) sums it up best. See also the entry on Cochran in the forthcoming biographical supplement to the *International Encyclopedia of the Social Sciences*.

18. This anomaly was first pointed out to me by Merritt Roe Smith. One of the best of the science, technology, and society programs is that at Lehigh University. Their "curriculum newsletter," entitled *Human Perspectives on Technology* and edited by Stephen H. Cutcliffe, has been very valuable.

19. This last matter, concerning contributions by the history of science, was forcefully pointed out to me by my colleague David Hounshell. My point here is *not* that the history of science and that of technology are unrelated—obviously they have extremely important and extensive interconnections, particularly in the twentieth century and most especially since 1945. Rather, I wish to maintain that there are and ought to be more extensive ties between business history and the history of technology than between the history of science and that of technology.

Something along these lines is hinted at in Nathan Rosenberg and Walter G. Vincente's *The Britannia Bridge: The Generation and Diffusion of Technological Knowledge* (Cambridge, Mass., 1978). "Engineers," they note, "are typically engaged in design activities in which they are subject to constraints of no particular interest to scientists. They are necessarily intensely concerned with financial considerations, for example, and their work in this respect is more closely related to economics than to the physical sciences." (p. 72).

20. The citation for this award, reported in *Isis*, the journal of the History of Science Society, noted that "Smith . . . may perhaps have been as surprised as historians of science will be to learn that his [book] has been awarded the Pfizer Prize, since neither science nor technology comprise the focus of his study. [!] However, this . . . book points the way to areas of scholarship that are likely to grow in importance as the history of science broadens as a discipline." *Isis* (March, 1979), 149.

21. The term "business history" has an imprecise meaning. To some extent, it covers the "old" economic history and the study of economic institutions, as well as the study of businesses. When I was editor of the *Business History Review*, I held to the catholic philosophy of my predecessor in that job, James P. Baughman, and published articles on a very wide range of topics, so long as they had some clear connection to business. Business history, Baughman maintained, was whatever appeared in the *Review*.

22. A chairman of the Association's membership committee referred to this as "the membership problem."

23. "Public history" generally refers to the work of those trained in history who pursue historical work in institutions other than colleges and universities, such as historical agencies and museums. There is now a journal, *The Public Historian*, published at the University of California, Santa Barbara.

24. In his preface to *Elmer Sperry*, Hughes acknowledges Chandler's strong intellectual influence.

25. This list could be extended greatly, but I will content myself with but a single further example, the work of Hugh G.J. Aitken. Though trained as an economist, Aitken is in many ways closer to the business-history wing of economic history than to the "new" economic history. His fine book *Taylorism at Watertown Arsenal* (Cambridge, Mass., 1960) has long been an important study for both historians of business and those of technology, and his ex-

cellent *Syntony and Spark—The Origins of Radio* (New York, 1976) represents a balanced blend of the history of science, technology, and industry. It won the Society for the History of Technology's Dexter Prize in 1976 and is a highly admirable, subtle, and sophisticated attempt to analyze the interconnections among science, technology, and the market.

26. These remarks are on the first page of his introduction to the Harbinger edition of *Technics and Civilization*.

Energy Flow in a Changing Economy, 1815-1880

Dolores Greenberg

Future generations may well look back on the decade of the 1970's as the beginning of a prolonged energy crisis that radically altered modern history. Faced with rising costs, fearing near-term scarcities, and anticipating the possible depletion of non-renewable fuels, industrialized as well as developing countries are deliberately poised at the transition to new energy systems. The 1980's are certain to be, as a Ford Foundation study urged, *A Time to Choose*,[1] and, as we know from the past, changes in harnessing, directing, and controlling energy can profoundly reshape socio-economic systems. It is surely the first time in this nation's history that the federal government has formally taken responsibility for initiating a change in energy supply and use patterns. To some observers, the assumption of energy policy decisions will prove a critical issue in a reversal of business-government relations that could lead, in the words of Robert Heilbroner, to the decline of business civilization.[2]

Our current concern over energy choices comes as the United States is approaching an unmarked centennial. It is just a hundred years since the transition from renewable energy sources to fossil fuels. In contrast to England, where coal and steam became synonymous with industrialization by the 1870's, only in the 1880's, a century later, did American energy patterns begin to reflect intensive use of fossil fuels. Bituminous and anthracite coal, both readily available by the 1840's, displaced renewable forms such as wood, water, and wind so slowly that in 1850 the use of mineral fuels accounted for less than 10 per cent of the energy derived from inanimate sources. After a further protracted delay of some thirty-five years, by 1885 the changeover to coal-fueled steam power and to coking coal in iron and steel manufactures finally raised the consumption of mineral fuels to just half the amount of energy harnessed from inanimate sources.[3]

More striking perhaps than the belated adoption of mineral fuels is the reliance at midcentury, or even by 1870, on animate sources of power. In keeping with energy flow patterns which went back thousands of years, draft animals and humans still served as the primary energy converters and still supplied the primary sources of motive power. The characteristic small-scale decentralized technologies for harnessing wind and water merely supplemented the work derived from humans, horses, oxen and mules. Even after the beginnings of big business, muscle power continued to account for the largest share of total power production.[4]

Here then was a nation where the decennial growth rate in manufacturing averaged 59 per cent between 1809 and 1839, and where, as Thomas Cochran has argued, "industrialization had by 1812 established a historical march of progress that was not to be turned back." The "critical point" of no return had already been passed by 1812, and certainly by 1850 the United States could be ranked with Great Britain in industrial eminence.[5] Yet whatever the changes in output, enterprise and infrastructure which in the first half of the century qualified the United States as a leading participant in the Industrial Revolution, there was a considerable lag in the development of what Lewis Mumford identified as a "paleotechnic society," a society in which technologies for converting coal, petroleum, and hydroelectric resources were not only readily available, but were also widely adopted.[6]

This curious phenomenon of United States reliance on renewable resources and muscle power to the virtual exclusion of fossil fuels for so much of the nineteenth century takes on added significance when set against the growing body of literature in which energy flows figure as key determinants of socio-cultural stability and change, social values, and levels of civilization.

Before turning to these complex relationships, we should first ask what energy is. In the modern world the word *energy* is most often used as an open–ended metaphor. It is variously equated with progress and productivity, or with engines, electricity, and nuclear power to reflect attitudes towards realized or potential technologies and resources. Although energy has many forms and sources the use of which depend ultimately on the constraints of social systems, by definition energy is the ability to do work. Power is the rate at which work is done, and heat, regarded as a special form of energy, is the equivalent of work as it brings about changes in temperature.

One of the more extraordinary discoveries of modern science was that the total energy in the universe is always constant. According to the first law of thermodynamics, when energy is converted from one form to another—say from the

kinetic energy of falling water or the chemical energy of food
to either mechanical or thermal energy—whatever the conversion process, energy neither can be created nor destroyed in
any observable process. It is because of this thermodynamic
law that all standard units for power, energy and work have
fixed mathematical relations. Although engineers commonly
speak of British thermal units, ecologists prefer kilocalories
and physicists joules, each is measuring energy and work in
units that can be converted from one to another.

So crucial has been the availability and actual use of
energy in human history that it has come to be regarded as a
causative factor in the evolution from simple horticultural
to advanced industrial society. There have been recurrent
analyses, especially since Lewis Mumford's *Technics and Civilization*, of the fundamental relationships between the types
of conversion processes (whether biochemical or technological) which enable societies to utilize the energy of the bio-
sphere and their many-faceted impacts on the development of
different civilizations. In a particularly influential study published in 1955, Fred Cottrell extended Mumford's thesis that
energy constitutes the principle resource shaping material
culture, applying it to an exploration of the interdependence
of energy technology, economic development, and social
change. Refining the concept of the physical economy of
energy, Cottrell posits the idea of surplus energy, "the energy
available to man in excess of that expended to make energy
available." His arguments relating energy surplus and scarcity
to value systems are placed in a historical framework to support his central claim that:

The energy available to man limits what he *can* and influences

what he *will* do ... [while] ... the preservation of a system of
values requires a continuous supply of energy equal to the de-
mands imposed by that system of values ... conversely changes
in amount and form of energy available give rise to conditions
likely to result in changes in values.[7]

Cottrell's work was supplemented by the studies of Leslie
White, Marshall Sahlins, E. R. Service, Dean Sheils, and
William Burch, among other anthropologists, ecologists, and
sociologists who present cultural change as the history of
increasing control over energy resources and power technologies. In these "thermodynamic," "neoevolutionary" interpre-
tations, the size, symbols, and complexity of social organizations, since the earliest periods of human history, are related
to the amounts of energy harnessed per capita, per annum.
The high consumption rate of fossil fuels in technologies for
generating increasing amounts of power is used as an "energetic" yardstick to distinguish modern industrial from less
developed societies. It is assumed that the development of
inanimate energy sources coupled to a dependence on increasing amounts of fossil fuels constitutes the underlying factor
responsible for rising levels of social welfare and individual
well being.[8]

These same theoretical references appear in the work of
economists and economic historians. Carlo Cipolla, for example, concluded that the more successfully man controls and
puts to use non-human energy, the "more he acquires control
over his environment and achieves goals other than those
strictly related to animal existence." David Landes set forth
what has been taken as the model for development when he
succinctly summarized the crucial components of the Industrial Revolution in England as "the substitution of machines

... for human skill and effort; the substitution of inanimate for animate sources of power, ... the substitution of mineral for vegetable or animal substances." American historians familiar with J. Frederick Dewhurst's standard study of *America's Needs and Resources* will note a similar set of criteria in his emphasis on the harnessing of vast amounts of inanimate energy "on a lavish scale to displace animal power and multiply human effort." More than either entrepreneurship or organization, Dewhurst presents use of fossil fuels as the crucial factor in the "fabulous" increase in output from 1850 to 1950. The chapter "Productivity: Key to Welfare" specifies how "our high productivity and high standard of living are in large part the fruits of a 'high-energy civilization.'"[9]

In terms of these criteria of energy flow analysis, the United States ranks, rather surprisingly, at the lower end of the development spectrum for much of the nineteenth century. During a period of rapid industrialization the nation relied, as societies had for 99.9 per cent of human history, on renewable organic resources to meet its energy needs.[10] As in today's lesser developed nations, plants and meat supplied the major sources of energy. Neither coal nor oil but rather food for humans and feed for animals constituted the basic fuel. Besides food, the remaining fuel basket was almost exclusively vegetable, with wood accounting for 90 per cent in 1850 and 75 per cent in 1870.[11]

Moreover, as noted earlier, until the 1880's and the proliferation of inanimate combustion engines, draft animals and humans acted as the most important energy converters and the major sources of power. Estimates of total horsepower of prime movers, even excluding humans, show that in 1850 work animals accounted for 6 million horsepower–hours as compared with 2.5 million for inanimate energy converters. A decade later work animals contributed 8.6 million hph, compared to 5.1 million for inanimate prime movers; by 1870 the amount supplied by work animals had climbed to 8.7 million hph, but inanimate converters contributed only 8.3 million.

Whether we are measuring horsepower shares of prime movers or the energy sources used for work output, the pattern is clear. The work obtained from animals alone exceeded the amounts derived from all inanimate sources until the third quarter of the nineteenth century.[12] Not until 1880 did the figures indicate a reversal, with the power produced by inanimate converters superseding that of work horses, oxen, and mules.[13]

Compared with muscle power, we might ask, what was the significance of fossil fuels and falling water, those sources most closely identified with America's industrialization? The data here are equally clear. Even when added together, the work output from these sources came to at most 15 per cent of the total derived from all nonfood energy sources in 1850, and by 1870 the figure still stood at about 33 per cent.[14] Moreover, according to what are judged "reasonable estimates," in 1850 "only about one-tenth of the total [nonfood] fuel supply was converted into mechanical energy, and, by 1870, approximately one-fifth was so utilized." Equally significant, considering the rapid rate of industrial advance and related innovation, is that the manufacturing and transportation sectors consumed only fractional amounts of energy from

TABLE I

Estimated Work Output, By Source of Energy, 1850-1900
(Billions of Horsepower-Hours)

Source of Energy	1850	1860	1870	1880	1890	1900
1. Total	10.3	15.4	19.0	29.9	48.2	78.5
2. Animate	6.8	9.4	10.5	13.9	17.9	21.0
3. Human workers	1.3	1.8	2.1	2.8	3.5	4.2
4. Work animals	5.4	7.6	8.4	11.1	14.4	16.9
5. Inanimate	3.6	5.9	8.5	16.0	30.3	57.6
6. Wind	1.4	2.1	1.1	1.1	1.0	1.0
7. Windmills	a	a	a	a	.1	.1
8. Sailing vessels	1.4	2.1	1.1	1.1	1.0	.9
9. Water	.9	1.3	1.7	2.0	2.2	3.3
10. Water wheels direct drive	.9	1.3	1.7	2.0	2.0	2.1
11. Hydroelectric	—	—	—	—	.2	1.2
12. Fuel	1.3	2.6	5.7	12.9	27.1	53.2
13. Minerals	.7	1.8	4.9	12.1	26.6	52.9
14. Bituminous	.4	1.0	3.0	9.3	22.5	48.1
15. Anthracite	.3	.9	1.9	2.8	4.0	4.2
16. Petroleum	—	—	—	—	—	.7
17. Natural Gas	—	—	—	—	—	.1
18. Fuel Wood	.6	.7	.8	.8	.5	.3

a. Less than .05.

TABLE II

Estimated Total Horsepower of All Prime Movers,
United States, 1849-1900
(thousands)

Year	Automotive	Total	Nonautomotive Work animals	Total Inanimate
1850		8,495	5,960	2,535
1860		13,763	8,630	5,133
1870		16,931	8,660	8,271
1880		26,314	11,580	14,734
1890		44,086	15,970	28,116
1900	100	64,945	18,730	46,215

From J. Frederick Dewhurst and Associates, *America's Needs and Resources: A New Survey.* Copyright © 1955 by the Twentieth Century Fund, Inc. Reprinted by permission.

the available inanimate sources.[15]

The data on energy composition and consumption reinforce Allen Pred's observation that as late as 1840 machine tools had not nearly superseded the use of hand tools in manufacturing: they underscore Nathan Rosenberg's point that mechanization did not depend on new power sources; and they also place in a somewhat different perspective the substitution processes which involve energy, work, and fossil fueled power technology as prerequisites for structural change.[16]

In addition to raising questions about commonly used energy criteria for appraising progress toward industrialization, the historical record reveals other surprises. It runs contrary to much current economic analysis in which it is assumed that rising levels of per capita energy consumption, in addition to reflecting levels of industrial advance, are also a prerequisite to increases in GNP. But again, judged by the American past, the idea that the more energy a nation uses the better off it will be proves as inadequate as the notion that energy use and GNP must run parallel, or that industrial societies necessarily consume more energy relative to GNP than agrarian societies. Quite the reverse occurred between 1850 and 1950. Total per capita energy consumption of mineral fuels, hydropower, and fuel wood increased less than one-half as much as per capita GNP. To put it another way, by 1880 energy consumption was at least one-third more in relation to GNP than in the highly industrialized United States of 1955.[17] In effect, we achieved considerable growth in GNP between 1880 and 1955 without comparable increases in the amounts of energy consumed.

These seeming paradoxes surrounding the relationship of

energy and economic change suggest that among the questions that need closer examination are why animate energy figured so prominently and for so long relative to inanimate energy, and why total energy consumption ranked so high. Involved is the nature and composition of energy supplies, the conversion efficiencies of energy technologies, and an analysis of what energy was used for.[18]

Although the word *energy* was not coined until 1807 and scientific principles governing energy use were not completely formulated even by 1850,[19] still Tench Coxe's report to Albert Gallatin on *Arts and Manufactures* in 1812 evidenced considerable insight into the relationship between different power sources, work and productivity. Coxe railed against ancient technological constraints that led to the hazards of human labor and made his report a plea for continued reductions in manpower, a word he used in the literal sense. His pivotal concern hinged on what we would call social costs, for as he observed, "the labor of many hands produces illness and disease," "sickly and deformed classes of people." To reduce these tangible costs he urged alternative supplementary power sources. Coxe's reflections on the effects of labor intensity led him to conceptualizations relating work, power and time, and he concluded that in addition to "corporal powers," Americans should adopt water, steam, machinery, chemistry, cattle, and horses.[20]

As we have become keenly aware, energy choices such as Coxe recommended involve an intricate mesh of resource availability, attitudes, technology, population patterns, and institutional structures, not to mention numerous economic and political variables. The utilization of energy in the nineteenth century, as today, also necessitated its transformation into needed forms, at appropriate locations, at acceptable social and economic costs. Finally, and fundamental to energy systems is the question of efficiency—the energy input required to produce a given amount of energy output.

What we find in the United States in the nineteenth century is a distinctive pattern of high consumption and low efficiency that can, at least in part, be explained by the continued use of wood, the single most important energy source aside from food until 1880. From the early colonial period the abundance of the American forests, the extraordinary stands of hickory, oak, and maple hardwood offered, as Charles Carroll has shown, a highly prized resource to Englishmen who had a recurrent history of fuel shortages and who in the early 17th century were again suffering from an acute energy crisis.[21] Good hardwood, thought to be as plentiful as air on the Eastern seaboard, seemed inexhaustible, and it has since been supposed that "wood was initially free and remained so for a large proportion of the rural population."[22]

The abundance of wood, nonetheless, as the Puritans perceived, bestowed a mixed blessing. Forests impeded cultivation, could harbor enemies, and at a spark could bring conflagration to whole communities.[23] Besides these costs, with dependence on existing technologies wood entailed high energy, high labor, and high economic costs. If in certain areas it was free for the taking, in a society where labor was scarce it proved expensive in both man hours and manpower. Because of its weight and bulk, the work it took to prepare hard, heavy, and bulky green cordwood became a common complaint on nineteenth-century family farms requiring some 20 cords a year. Cutting was done by hand with very simple tools, and the most a skilled axman could cut, haul, saw to size, split, and stack totaled at best a cord a day. A less skilled worker would take two to three days to complete the job. By 1850, when animal power had replaced human labor for many farm chores, sawing and splitting continued to be done exclusively with hand-held tools.[24] The labor intensity of fuel wood preparation interested a government expert some 70 years later, and he noted, in studying the fuel shortages of 1917 and 1918, that fuel wood still required more labor than coal production.[25] Yet another disadvantage which might have been noted is that a cord of dried hardwood, which weighs twice as much as a ton of coal, contains only 80 per cent of the heat value.

Reliance on wood fuel clearly contributed to energy intensiveness. And if we were to calculate the ratios in an energy budget beginning with the measure of caloric intake necessary for labor input, we would in all probability also find that more food fuel (in the form of kilocalories) was required to prepare wood fuel than was derived (in the form of Btu's) from its end-uses.[26] Paradoxically too, dependence on wood fuel, in a society short of labor, encouraged its inefficient utilization, which in turn resulted in high overall energy consumption levels.

A sectoral breakdown of end-use reveals the problem. In 1850, households consumed 90 per cent of all wood fuel: 15 per cent went for cooking, drying, smoking, and process heat for home manufactures; the remainder, 75 per cent, was burned for space heating in large open fireplaces. These typically functioned at such low thermal efficiencies that 80 per cent of the heat went up the chimney. Yet the general public could little afford to pay attention to experiments in the late 1820's — presuming they knew of them — which demonstrated that fireplaces used four times more wood to heat a given area, and perhaps, as some Georgia experiments showed, ten times more than enclosed stoves. Manpower considerations figured as a more immediate factor and retarded adoption of this more heat efficient technology in many rural areas. Where wood was plentiful, why spend extra time sawing and splitting much smaller pieces to fit the interiors of enclosed stoves? Elsewhere, price was the consideration. Even in rural New England, where wood scarcities had been reflected in prices as early as 1700, as well as in the rapidly growing cities of the Northeast, where smokeless anthracite had begun to replace wood in fireplace grates by the 1820's, stoves were not generally adopted until the 1850's.[27] A scarcity of iron coupled to poor transportation contributed to the sluggish commercial development of stove manufactures, and these bulky items— priced by the pound—remained too expensive for widespread household adoption.[28]

If, on the one hand, wood-fuel production demanded high levels of energy input, and on the other, the bulk of it was utilized for space heating at low thermal efficiencies, we should also note that very little was converted to mechanical energy to replace muscle power. Wood did figure in the transportation sector as an important source of heat and power in 1850 and, in fact, well into the 1880's. Steam engines, especially for steamboats and locomotives, were fired principally by wood until a decline set in by the 1890's. Stationary engines for steam-plows and steam-drawn threshing machines had also appeared by the 1850's in agriculture.[29] We can, of course, point to the fact that in industry one-half of the iron output was smelted with charcoal from dried eastern hardwoods in 1850, and to obtain two tons of charcoal required eight tons of wood. Compared to household use, however, the aggregates consumed in transportation and industry remained small. We have detailed records for 1870 showing that households consumed 75 per cent of wood-fuel supplies and industrial use came to only 4.5 per cent. To put it another way, we can say that the heat of wood fuel was not converted, in any significant amounts, into motive power. At most, 10 million cords, from an annual production of 140 million, were converted to meechanical energy in 1870.[30]

On the one hand, then, we have the fact that wood supplied over 90 per cent of non-food fuel in 1850 and 75 per cent in 1870, and on the other hand we know that utilization of large proportions was linked to inefficient conversion technologies. Together these factors explain why the efficiency of energy conversion for all sources is estimated at a low of 6 to 8 per cent in these decades, and why the levels of energy consumption in agrarian America were so anomalously high.[31] In 1850, for example, per capita annual energy consumption in the United States, even excluding water and wind power, is estimated at 100 million British thermal units, a level not reached in Great Britain until 1865, and not reached in Germany until World War I.[32]

Such comparative consumption data underscore the importance of efficiencies in analyzing the relationships between

energy and output or energy and industrial advance. In
neither case is there a one-to-one linkage which would allow
classification of cultures, economic development, or levels of
well-being based simply on estimates of total per capita kilocalories or Btu's. We should be suspect of broad generalizations and overarching conclusions which posit that "advances
from one state of society to the next are marked . . . by large
increases in the rate of energy use."[33]

Equally questionable, moreover, is the complementary
proposition that the industrializing process invariably initi-
ates significant improvements in the efficiency of energy
systems.[34] Certainly, it is difficult to reconcile the American
record with attempts to classify societies in terms of energy
efficiencies. According to such rankings, advanced agricultural societies are characterized by aggregate energy efficiencies of 15 per cent; the energy systems of emerging industrial
societies are pegged at 25 per cent; and the aggregate efficiency of energy systems in advanced industrial-technological
societies is supposed to reach a minimum of 36 per cent.[35]
When compared with these guidelines, however, the United
States figures in fact indicate a decline in energy efficiency
from 8.2 per cent in 1850 to 4.4 per cent in 1900. By 1950,
the figure had climbed to only 13.8 per cent, and the high of
38 per cent was not achieved until 1969.[36]

During the nineteenth-century, as we have seen, wood use
incurred such gross inefficiencies that it can account for the
overall statistics, at least until 1870, when its consumption
peaked nationally. But the subsequent declines in aggregate
efficiency over the next thirty years also reflect other factors,
including the energy losses of technologies designed to obtain

TABLE III

Estimated Efficiency of Energy Conversion, By Source of Energy, 1850-1950

(per cent)

Year	All Sources	Inanimate Energy				
		All Sources	Fuels and Water Power	Minerals and Water Power	Minerals	Bituminous, Anthracite, Nat. Gas, Fuel Wood
1850	8.2	3.0	1.8	2.4	1.1	1.1
1860	7.4	3.0	2.0	2.2	1.3	1.3
1870	5.8	2.7	2.3	2.4	1.8	1.8
1880	5.2	2.8	2.6	2.7	2.3	2.3
1890	4.5	2.9	2.8	2.8	2.6	2.6
1900	4.4	3.2	3.2	3.2	3.0	3.0
1910	5.4	4.7	4.7	4.6	4.4	4.4
1920	7.9	7.4	7.4	7.4	7.0	7.0
1930	12.7	12.3	12.3	12.3	11.8	13.6
1940	13.5	13.2	13.2	13.2	12.6	16.3
1950	13.8	13.6	13.6	13.6	12.9	18.5

From J. Frederick Dewhurst and Associates, *America's Needs and Resources: A New Survey.* Copyright © 1955 by the Twentieth Century Fund, Inc. Reprinted by permission.

process heat and work in the industrial sector.

Just as gains in energy efficiency, while ultimately critical for societies dependent on non-renewable fossil fuels, clearly cannot be counted as a standard byproduct of the industrializing process, so we should note that gains in per capita output are not necessarily linked to energy efficiency. Like energy input and GNP, there is no certain correlation. The fact that per capita increases in output took place more rapidly and readily than energy efficiencies in the early nineteenth-century helps to clarify the conceptual differences and emphasizes the need for placing energy use patterns of the past in their structural context. In the colonial era, for example, when manufactures were at the handicraft stage and product figured more importantly than productivity, output remained more closely related to skill than to the rate at which work was done. Of course the adoption of even the simplest hand-held tools helped to extend the meager power capabilities of the human body, resulting in gains in product output. Adoption of basic devices of power technology did not, however, also increase the actual energy output of the body, the efficiency of the body as an energy converter, or the total amounts of energy available to society. So wherever heavy jobs required more energy than could be furnished by the limits of human muscle, then animals, wind, and water power were harnessed for useful work.

Falling water of course had supplied direct power for manufacturing from the early colonial period. Dams built with local materials by local labor dotted the rivers and streams of the East, and these small-scale installations furnished power for grist mills, saw mills, flour mills, and iron fabrication. If the theoretical dimensions of energy conversion eluded colonial millwrights, they were more interested in controversies over practical matters of cost, design, and relative waterwheel performance, especially as mills became the centers of expanded economic opportunity.[37] By the eighteenth-century watermills counted so heavily in calculations of community prosperity that this private service came gradually to be regarded as a public responsibility needing government protection and encouragement. New York formalized the relationship and created the first public service energy corporations, when the state allowed all mills de facto corporate powers in 1735.[38]

The many-faceted economic importance of milling operations, including their contributions to power output and productivity, is in no way diminished by the fact that until water turbines were adopted in the 1850's, waterwheels could convert to useful work only a fraction of the energy applied to them. The energy efficiency of the typical vertical wheel is estimated at about 5 per cent, while the efficiency with which animate converters such as humans and animals transferred chemical energy to work is estimated in the range of 20 to 30 per cent. In breaking the limitations of power characteristic of humans and animals, waterwheels increased the flow of goods and services without making any major breakthroughs in energy efficiencies. Similarly, too, the early locomotives, whether using coal or wood, were nowhere as energy-efficient as horses. These locomotives offered greater speed and power, but their energy conversion efficiency is rated at most at 2 per cent compared to 20 per cent for a horse.[39]

An Anglo-American comparison further emphasizes that ratios of energy efficiency reflect availability, the energy mix, and intensity rather than levels of economic development. For clearly, the use of energy and the search for power in the industrial sector generated a strikingly different sequence in the United States and England. Until the Civil War and after, water power sites determined factory and urban location; water-milling enterprises linked rural agrarian hinterlands to the market economy; and waterwheels directly powered the rapidly growing light industry of New England and the mid-Atlantic states. Louis Hunter's reappraisal of the relative roles of water and steam in the American experience leaves little doubt as to the importance or the appropriateness of this low-cost, decentralized technology for the nation's industrial development.[40]

In contrast to England, wood fuel shortages intensified dependence on water power. Although similar scarcities brought a transition to coal, coke, and steam in England, in New England the depletion of 8 million acres of woodland coincided with the introduction of power driven textile looms so that falling water became the most obvious and best energy choice. For manufacturers faced with the urgency of the crisis, steam engines or "other modes of operation requiring fire" were a costly if not quixotic alternative, considering the poor distribution network in 1815.[41] As contemporaries were well aware, the scarcity in New England had to be viewed as a regional bottleneck since the spread and diversity of the energy mix would insure different solutions for different uses in other areas. And wood did continue to be available for charcoal smelting while water power was so widely adopted in the next fifty years as to account for almost half of installed horsepower in manufacturing by 1869.[42] In other words, energy availability which allowed acceleration in the growth of productivity removed the need for a parallel acceleration in the efficiency of energy use.

Although waterwheels harnessing the force of rivers and streams supplied mechanical energy for 150 years in the United States before the more efficient French-designed turbines came into use in the 1850's, by then the relative importance of water as a source of inanimate power had already begun to peak owing to the gradual adoption of coal. Wind in fact provided more horsepower in 1850 than water, although together they supplied 65 per cent of inanimate motive force.[43] By 1870 a dramatic decline became evident with wind and water accounting for only 33 per cent of inanimate mechanical power. In terms of our larger frame of reference, however, we should note that mineral fuels and falling water still supplied less useful energy than muscles, a situation which contrasts markedly with the model for industrialization.[44]

The belated adoption of coal in an interlinked process of innovation and diffusion of new technology in manufacturing and transportation only partially explains the contrast in overall energy patterns between the United States and England. Obviously, agriculture constituted the largest sector of the American economy employing the largest number of people, and energy flows in this area had the greatest impact on aggregate energy efficiencies as well as on the relationship between energy and output. As we might expect, in agriculture as in industry remarkably little change took place in basic fuels for most of the nineteenth century. Until 1820 and even into the 1840's a combination of inertia and adherence to traditional behavior also retarded adoption of new methods or improved implements.[45] The sources of power similarily stayed constant so that in 1850, when 5.1 million draft animals supplied 2.6 billion hph, the power of animals was just beginning to provide a significant replacement for manpower and two decades later energy inputs continued to be derived almost exclusively from the sun, the wind, and muscle power.[46] In sum, the postwar trend toward mechanization and increased productivity in agriculture had not been accompanied by simultaneous changes to inanimate from animate sources of power, by the substitution of mineral for vegetable fuels, or by the large-scale replacement of men by machines.

In terms of "energetic" criteria, agriculture, like industry, ranked at the lower end of the development spectrum. On the other hand, in contrast to industry, or for that matter in contrast to modern fossil-fuel intensive farming, nineteenth-century food production, categorized as pre-industrial, was highly energy efficient.

An explanation for this phenomenon can be illuminated by reference to the report of Joseph Kennedy, Superintendent of the Census, who in 1864 set down his observations on the use of machinery in agriculture.[47] Kennedy touched on what have become key areas of examination in bioenergetic research: the relationship between energy, labor, land use, and food production. His analysis, offered as a defense of the American system of agriculture, focused on how methods of cultivation, manuring, and mechanization effected work savings and low labor inputs. He justified the American farmers' reliance on the nutrients obtained from scattered ashes, natural carbonic acids, and ammonia from the atmosphere, just as he applauded the migration to virgin lands. Extensive rather than intensive agriculture, like the use of natural fertilizer, was, he argued, the best labor-saving response where land is rich and labor scarce. And in calling for continued utilization of mechanical devices, he emphasized what was the central pre-occupation of the period—the ability to do work and the rate at which work was done.

In many ways these conceptions had more immediacy in the nineteenth century than they have today. The slow uneven transition from humans to horses, from hand tools to machines, provoked ongoing analyses of the process and value of work that were central to metaphysical speculation at the same time that they were the substance of government reports. In this case, it is striking that for all of Kennedy's enthusiasm for the "vast power resident in machinery" that could be "increased beyond computation by the use of steam as a prime mover," his catalogue of favored innovations adopted since the London Exhibition of 1851 makes clear that machines still served mainly as extensions of animal or human muscle.[48] Although, as he said, the rude plow of the Hebrew prophets had been continually improved, nevertheless the rotary spade was preferred over the steam plow and it depended on horse power, as did the two-horse hay rake, and horse-powered theshing, reaping, and mowing machines.

As long as labor savings could be linked to an expanding area of cultivation, mechanization could continue to be dependent on animate sources of power and still result in increases of productivity to meet market demand. Kennedy was correct on two points: that these methods would have to be altered once new lands could no longer be brought

into cultivation; and that until then extensive farming was
cheaper in terms of labor input than intensive agriculture.
Ironically, according to recent calculations of energy expended, food-raising using these techniques of hand cultivation and animal-powered production are much more energy
efficient than modern mechanized agriculture using fossil
fuels. Gerald Leach had reviewed a number of new studies
which reveal the high energy needs of modern food production and notes that by contrast "nearly all pre-industrial farmers and food gathers achieve very large energy returns on
the work they put in. The Energy Ratio (Er) which measures
the edible energy output divided by the energy input, is much
higher than for any industrial farming system, while the use
of fossil fuels is zero or very small."[49]

The United States stands, then, as an example of a nation
which achieved significant rates of economic growth although
relying on energy-inefficient technology in manufacturing, and
on muscle power, water, wind, and wood to the virtual exclusion of fossil fuels until the 1870's. At the current moment,
when many industrializing nations are searching for appropriate energy paths based on indigenous supplies, our experience may provide the basis for reappraising assumptions
concerning the massive application of nonrenewable resources during the developmental stages of industrialization,
as well as a fresh appreciation of the relationship between
energy and GNP. Without question, the differing energy patterns in the United States during the transition to modern
industrialism amply demonstrates the complexities of energy
flows and brings into question simple hypotheses which take

for granted increasing consumption rates of fossil fuels as prerequisites for progress. The record suggests too the value of systematic analysis which measures energy efficiencies as against economic efficiencies. Use of energy budgeting methods would help to further clarify these variables of economic growth and the interaction between humans and their resource environment.

1. Energy Policy Project, Ford Foundation, *A Time to Choose* (Cambridge, Mass., 1974).

2. Robert Heilbroner, *Business Civilization in Decline* (New York, 1976), 101–113. For a review of arguments linking contemporary energy choices to structural change, see Amory Lovins, *Soft Energy Paths* (Cambridge, Mass., 1977), 147–157.

3. For England see David S. Landes, *The Unbound Prometheus* (Cambridge, Mass., 1969) 95–104, 215–21. For the United States see Sam H. Schurr and Bruce Netschert, *Energy in the American Economy, 1850-1955* (Baltimore, 1960), 31–44, 57–67; Peter Temin, *The Jacksonian Economy* (New York, 1969), 163 ff; Temin, *Iron and Steel in Nineteenth-Century America* (Cambridge, Mass., 1964); see also Temin, "Steam and Waterpower in the Early Nineteenth Century," *Journal of Economic History,* (June, 1966), 187 ff; Louis C. Hunter, "The Heavy Industries Before 1869," Harold F. Williamson, ed., *The Growth of the American Economy* (New York, 1955), 155 ff; Alfred D. Chandler, Jr., "Anthracite Coal and the Beginnings of the Industrial Revolution in the United States," *Business History Review,* XLVI (Summer, 1972), 141–81.

4. See table I. I rely on Dewhurst's estimates of 1955. The pattern would be even bolder if, as William Burch, I had chosen Dewhurst's earlier figures of 1948 which indicate the distribution of energy output for mineral fuels and falling water as 5.8 per cent in 1850; 6.5 per cent in 1860; 11.5 per cent in 1870; and 17.2 per cent in 1880. According to these same estimates the work derived from humans and animals came to 95.2 per cent in 1850; 93.5 in 1860; 88.5 per cent in 1870 and 83.8 per cent in 1880. Moreover, it wasn't until the 1900's that mineral fuels and falling water superseded muscular power in these estimates of national energy production. For an interesting analysis of resource limits, see William Burch, Jr., "Resources and Social Structure: Some Conditions of Stability and Change," *The Annals,* 389 (May, 1973), 27–34.

5. W. Elliot Brownlee, *Dynamics of Ascent: A History of the American Economy* (New York, 1974), 86; Thomas C. Cochran, "An Analytical View of Early American Business and Industry," in *Business Enterprise in Early New York,* Joseph Frese, S.J. and

Jacob Judd, eds. (New York, 1979), 1–13.

6. Lewis Mumford, *Techniques and Civilization* (New York, 1934).

7. Fred W. Cottrell, *Energy and Society* (Westport, Conn., 1970), 2, 11–12 ff.

8. See especially Leslie White, *The Evolution of Culture* (New York, 1959); Marshall D. Sahlins and E. R. Service, *Evolution and Culture* (Ann Arbor, Mich., 1960); E. R. Service, *Cultural Evolutionism* (New York, 1971). Dean Sheils analyzes the role of energy in neoevolutionary theory in "The Importance of Agriculture from the Perspective of Neoevolutionary Theory," *Rural Sociology,* 37 (1972), 167–188.

9. Carlo Cipolla, *The Economic History of World Population* (Baltimore, 1962), 35–36; Landes, *Prometheus Unbound,* 1; J. Frederick Dewhurst and Associates, *America's Needs and Resources* (New York, 1955) 902–905 ff., 943.

10. Earl Cook, *Man, Energy and Society* (San Francisco, 1976), 55; Chauncery Starr, "Energy and Power," *Scientific American* (September, 1971), reprinted in *Energy and Power* (San Francisco, 1971), 3–15, a very useful collection of *Scientific American* articles on energy.

11. Schurr and Netschert, *Energy in the American Economy,* 45–47; R. V. Reynolds and Albert H. Pierson, *Fuel Wood Use in the United States, 1630-1930,* United States Department of Agriculture, Forest Service Circular No. 641 (Washington, D.C., 1942), 8.

12. Using Dewhurst's data, Schurr and Netschert estimate that the work output from all inanimate energy sources in 1850 totalled 3.6 billion hph compared to 5.4 billion hph for the work output of draft animals. In 1860 the figures for work output are 5.9 billion hph from inanimate energy sources and 7.6 billion hph from animals; for 1870 the data are 8.5 billion hph for inanimate sources and 8.4 billion hph for animals. *Energy in the American Economy,* 55.

13. See Table II.

14. See Table I.

15. Schurr and Netschert, *Energy in the American Economy,* 51; Dewhurst, *America's Needs and Resources,* 1114–1115; Palmer Putnam, *Energy in the Future* (New York, 1953), 83–89.

16. Allan R. Pred, *The Spatial Dynamics of United States Urban-Industrial Growth, 1800-1914* (Cambridge, Mass., 1973), 117–34, and especially the analysis of interurban innovation diffusion, 239–83. Nathan Rosenberg, *Technology and American Economic Growth* (New York, 1972), 62–75, 157–59.

17. For a review of current approaches and critical analyses of the relationship of energy to GNP, see Joel Darmstadter, *How Industrial Societies Use Energy* (Baltimore, 1977), 1–34; Lovins, *Soft Energy Paths*, part I. According to one estimate, GNP per capita rose sixfold from the early 1850's to 1950, while energy use per capita about doubled. *A Time to Choose*, 17. For another supporting estimate see Schurr and Netschert, *Energy in the American Economy*, 157.

18. S. W. Angrist and L. G. Helper, *Order and Chaos, Laws of Energy and Entropy* (New York, 1967), 10–15; Cook, *Man, Energy and Society*, 32–33; D.S.L. Cardwell, *From Watt to Clausius* (Ithaca, N.Y., 1971) explain the history and concepts of thermodynamics.

19. For standard energy conversion equivalencies such as a horsepower hour, the kilowatt hour, or for measurements of heat content, such as a Btu, see Dewhurst, *America's Needs and Resources*, 1101.

20. Tench Coxe, *A Statement of the Arts and Manufactures of the United States of America* (1812), xxi, xxiv-xxv; Coxe, *Supplementary Observations* (1814) liv-lv.

21. Charles Carroll, *The Timber Economy of Puritan New England* (Providence, 1973), 1–70; Carroll, "The Forest Society of New England," in Brooke Hindle, ed., *America's Wooden Age; Aspects of its Early Technology* (Tarrytown, N.Y., 1975), 15.

22. *Ibid.*, 11.

23. Carroll, *Timber Economy*, 58–63; Peter N. Carroll, *Puritanism and the Wilderness: The Intellectual Significance of the New England Frontier, 1629-1700* (New York, 1969), 181–96. Even during the fuel crisis of 1812 Tench Coxe observed that forests prevent cultivation, but he went on to urge that the areas' wood could serve many regional needs for increasing "the prosperity of the landed interests." Coxe, *Arts and Manufactures*, lviii.

24. Reynolds and Pierson, *Fuel Wood Use*, 1–11.
25. Henry S. Graves, *The Use of Wood for Fuel*, U.S. Department of Agriculture Bulletin No. 753 (Washington, D.C., 1919), 2. By 1923 concern over forest exhaustion, linked to the high cost of lumber, replaced worries over coal scarcity. See R. V. Reynolds and Albert H. Pierson, *Lumber Cut of the United States, 1870-1920*, U.S. Department of Agriculture Bulletin No. 1119 (Washington, D.C., 1923), 1–24.
26. Energy accounting methodological tools have been developed for determining the amounts of energy expenditure needed for specific types of jobs. See, for example, Daniel Gross and Barbara Underwood, "Technological Change and Caloric Costs: Sisal Agriculture in Northeastern Brazil, *American Anthropologist*, 73 (June, 1971), 725–39; Gerald Leach, *Energy and Food Production* (Surrey, 1976).
27. Reynolds and Pierson, *Fuel Wood Use*, 3–11; Nathan Rosenberg, "America's Rise to Woodworking Leadership," *America's Wooden Age*, 54.
28. For postwar difficulties in the stove industry and the goals of the newly formed trade association, see *A Report of the Proceedings at the First Semi-Annual Meeting of the Stove Manufacturers of the United States*, (Albany, N.Y., 1872).
29. Schurr and Netschert, *Energy in the American Economy*, 52–54; Louis C. Hunter, *Steamboats on the Western Rivers* (Cambridge, Mass., 1949), 33 ff. Joseph Kennedy's report in 1864 extolling the use of machinery in agriculture noted that the Illinois Central premium for use of the steam plow in 1855 did little to encourage adoption. Joseph G. Kennedy, *Agriculture of the United States in 1860* (Washington, D.C., 1864), xv, xix.
30. Schurr and Netschert, *Energy in the American Economy*, 52–53; Putnam, *Energy in the Future*, 101–05.
31. See Table III.
32. Putnam, *Energy in the Future*, 340–62, 371–88.
33. Cook, *Man, Energy and Society*, 134.
34. Cook, *Ibid*. See Claude M. Summers, "The Conversion of Energy," *Energy and Power*, 95–106, for a discussion of the principles of energy efficiency.
36. See Table III; Putnam, *Energy in the Future*, 86–92, 368–70.

37. Charles Howell, "Colonial Watermills in the Wooden Age," *America's Wooden Age*, 134, 143–59.
38. Joseph A. Pratt, "The Public Service Origins of the American Business Corporation," *Business History Review*, lii (Spring, 1978), 36.
39. Cook, *Man, Energy and Society*, 28, 30, 135; Starr, "Energy and Power," *Energy and Power*, 1–8; Summers, "The Conversion of Energy," *Energy and Power*, 95–99; Rosenberg, *Technology and American Economic Growth*, 65–66.
40. Louis C. Hunter, "Waterpower in the Century of the Steam Engine," *America's Wooden Age*, 160–202.
41. Coxe, *Arts and Manufactures*.
42. Schurr and Netschert, *Energy in the American Economy*, 55.
43. *Ibid.*, 54.
44. See Table I.
45. Clarence Danhof, *Changes in Agriculture in the Northern United States, 1820-1870* (Cambridge, Mass., 1969), 75–84.
46. See Table I.
47. Kennedy, *Agriculture of the United States*.
48. *Ibid.*, xi.
49. Leach, *Energy and Food Production*, 7; Roy A. Rappaport, "The Flow of Energy in an Agricultural Society," *Energy and Power*, 69–80; David Pimental, *et al.*, "Food Production and the Energy Crisis," 182, *Science* (1973), 443–49.

Canals and Turnpikes:
America's Early-Nineteenth-Century Transportation Network

John F. Stover

In the half-century after the inauguration of George Washington, no country faced problems of transportation greater than those confronting the young United States. In the last years of the eighteenth century, transportation, both in Europe and America, was still geared to the speed of the horse, and was little, if any, faster than that known 1,800 years before in the days of Julius Caesar. In fact, the terrible condition of most roads meant that American transport was generally inferior to Roman. In the early nineteenth century the young nation was expanding to such an extent that talk of the Louisiana Purchase and the Pacific beyond held little real meaning for the average citizen. Before long, the growing nation stretched 3,000 miles to the far Pacific, a vast area soon to be filling with people. Between 1790 and 1850 the population of the nation increased nearly sixfold. The population was soon agitating for improvements in transportation. Taverns and exchanges across the broad land heard the warm arguments of farmers, merchants, and politicians as they advanced the rival claims of turnpikes and canals, of steamboats and railroads.

Citizens and political leaders alike were infused with a

desire for internal improvements. Both Thomas Jefferson and
his Secretary of the Treasury, Albert Gallatin, sponsored extensive plans for long-range public improvements. A few
years later Henry Clay in his "American System" placed
much emphasis upon improved roads and projected canals.
In 1817 John C. Calhoun, at the time a nationalist leader and
a supporter of the Bonus Bill for internal improvements, said:
"We are great, and rapidly—I was about to say fearfully—
growing. This is our pride and danger, our weakness and our
strength. . . . Let us, then, bind the republic together with a
perfect system of roads and canals."[1]

Certainly a "perfect system of roads and canals" did not
exist in 1817. While scores of turnpikes had been started by
that year, many were not yet completed. The completion of the
National, or Cumberland, Road to Wheeling on the Ohio
River came only in 1818, and the first Concord coach would
not be built for a decade. In 1817 the total mileage of canals
in America was no more than 100 miles, and the longest, the
Middlesex north of Boston, had a length of less than 28 miles.
It was in April, 1817, that final approval for the construction
of the Erie Canal was given by the New York legislature.
Only a handful of steamboats were operating on western
rivers in 1817, and the first successful railroads in the nation
were more than a decade in the future.[2]

Both turnpikes and canals were to increase greatly in the
first half of the nineteenth century. Between the building of
the Philadelphia–Lancaster Turnpike in the 1790's and the
decline of the boom in the 1830's, hundreds of turnpikes were
projected and built in the northeastern states. Probably a total
of 12,000 miles of toll roads were completed in those years,

with the great bulk of the mileage located in New England,
New York, and Pennsylvania. Very few such roads were built
west of Ohio or south of Virginia. The boom in canals came a
little later. The canal system in the nation grew from 100
miles in 1817 to 1,200 miles in 1830, about 3,300 miles in
1840, and 3,700 miles in 1850. In 1850 twenty different states
possessed canals, but more than two-thirds of the mileage was
located in the three states of Pennsylvania, New York, and
Ohio. Very few canals were found west of Indiana or south of
Virginia. New York State led all the states in turnpike mileage, and while bowing to Pennsylvania in canal mileage,
could claim that the Erie Canal was the busiest and most
profitable man-made waterway in the nation.[3]

The idea for turnpikes first appeared in England, when
Parliament, early in the reign of Charles II, authorized a private company to improve and maintain a specified piece of
road and to charge tolls for its use. However, such activity in
England did not become common until the Industrial Revolution in the middle decades of the eighteenth century required
improved transportation.[4] The first toll roads in America were
established during the late 1780's. The state legislature of
Virginia passed an act in 1785 providing for the collection of
tolls on certain public roads leading into Alexandria. The fees
collected at the tollgates—or turnpikes as they were originally
called—were to provide for the repair and maintenance of the
designated roads. Two years later, in 1787, Maryland set up
a similar program for several roads running west out of Baltimore. These early state-sponsored improved toll roads were
not very successful.

Travel on American roads was not easy in the last years of

the eighteenth century. When Christopher Colles made his survey of coastal roads of the mid-Atlantic region in the late 1780's, he found them to be in terrible condition. Washington's trip from Mount Vernon to New York City in April, 1789, was certainly delayed by the crowds of people who wished to cheer the President-elect. But his coach was also delayed by the rough and rutted roads. South of the Potomac the roads were even more primitive. In 1801, twelve years after Washington's trip, the third President, Thomas Jefferson, had to cross eight streams in his journey from Monticello to Washington, D.C. Only three of the eight streams could be crossed by bridge. When a traveler from abroad, Isaac Weld, Jr., journeyed through Maryland in 1795, he claimed the roads of that state to be the worst in the nation. He recalled one road so bad that "The driver frequently had to call to the passengers in the stage to lean out of the carriage first on one side, then on the other, to prevent it from oversetting in the deep ruts with which the road abounds. . . ."[5]

Hauling freight on such roads was very expensive. Five dollars was often charged for carrying a barrel of flour 150 miles. Salt, which sold for a penny a pound along the coast, might sell for 6 cents a pound 300 miles inland, the increase being the cost of transportation. Much farm produce could not be moved to market because of high transport costs.[6] Only those goods high in value or low in weight could be profitably shipped with such freight rates. Thus the wagon freight moving from Philadelphia or Baltimore to Pittsburgh chiefly consisted of gunpowder, ironware, cloth, boots, hats, and leather goods.

The first successful American turnpike was the Philadel-

phia and Lancaster Turnpike, running westward from Philadelphia a distance of 62 miles. In April, 1792, the Philadelphia promoters of the road received a charter from the state
legislature, which was already spending several thousand
dollars a year on the public roads of the state. The promoters
of the new turnpike quickly sold a thousand shares of stock at
$300 a share. It was not surprising that Philadelphians should
grow excited about improving transportation. First in population among American cities, Philadelphia claimed the nation's
first daily newspaper, saw its foreign trade increase fourfold
in the five years after 1791, and soon would build a city
water system.[7]

The 62-mile turnpike from Philadelphia to Lancaster was
started in 1792 and completed two years later. The total cost
of construction was $465,000, or $7,500 per mile. The road
was twenty-four feet wide with a maximum grade of about
four per cent. It was hard-surfaced, paved with stone and
overlaid with gravel. Travelers enjoyed the smooth ride, and
the young Englishman Francis Baily spoke of the new turnpike as a "masterpiece of its kind." Nine tollgates were placed
along the road, located 3 to 10 miles apart. Tolls were charged
by the mile, and empty wagons passed at half the charge for
loaded ones. More than forty items were included in the toll
list. A score of cattle cost 2.5 cents a mile, while a one-horse
two-wheel cart cost but 1.25 cents a mile. Business was brisk,
and by the turn of the century annual toll revenues were up to
$20,000 or more. Albert Gallatin calculated that annual oper-
ating expenses came to about $13,250, including yearly wages
of $250 to $350 for each tollgate keeper and road repairs of
$8,000 a year. Annual dividends paid stockholders averaged

only 2 per cent a year up to 1803, but the president of the Lancaster Turnpike, Elliston Perot, was confident that dividends would soon be up to 4 or 5 per cent. In any event, the heavy traffic on the new road soon inspired many other promoters to plan and build additional turnpikes.[8]

The longest, best-known, and most expensive turnpike in the United States was the National Road. In the Enabling Act of 1802, passed by Congress to allow the people of the Ohio Territory to seek statehood, a clause was added providing that 5 per cent of land sale proceeds should be used for the building of roads, with a portion to be spent on a route from navigable eastern rivers to the Ohio River and the new state of Ohio. President Jefferson appointed a committee which recommended a route from Cumberland, Maryland, across the mountains of Maryland and Pennsylvania to Wheeling, Virginia, on the Ohio River, Jefferson signed the National Road Bill on March 29, 1806, but contracts for construction were not let until 1811. The act provided for a cleared right of way four rods wide, with a central raised carriageway of stone and gravel. Construction during the War of 1812 was delayed, but the entire 130-mile road was completed to Wheeling by 1818. As each section was completed it was quickly opened to public use. No tolls were charged on any part of the road in the early years of its operation, even though the construction up to 1818 had cost the federal government over $1.5 million. East of Cumberland good connecting roads gave service into Baltimore. Travel on the new road was soon brisk, with mail coaches, stagecoaches, Conestoga wagons, and westward-moving settlers all crowding the road. The Philadelphia merchant-traveler John Melish called the new route "the finest road in the world," and *Niles' Weekly Register* was soon reporting that congressmen could now travel to and from their western homes at the rate of a hundred miles a day.[9]

The heavy traffic changed Wheeling from a struggling settlement on the eastern bank of the Ohio to a bustling town soon to have brick buildings and paved streets. The Wheeling *Gazette* started to brag about the hundreds of freight wagons that arrived from the East each season; and soon the merchants of Pittsburgh were complaining about the traffic lost to their rival down the Ohio. The heavy traffic was hard on the National Road, and by the winter of 1822–23 Postmaster General Return J. Meigs was reporting that much of the route was in a ruinous condition because of ruts and rock slides. Certainly most of the government money had gone for construction rather than repairs or maintenance. Congress in the middle 1820's provided for the westward extension of the National Road, now known as the "Old Pike," and by 1833 the road had been built to Columbus, Ohio, and by 1850 completed across Indiana. Long before this, sections had been turned over to the individual control of states, each of which generally started to collect tolls. By 1838 the federal government had spent nearly $7 million on the National Road.[10]

Inspired by the early success of the Lancaster Turnpike and the involvement of the federal government in building the National Road, more and more states became interested in building turnpikes. The great bulk of such activity came in the first third of the nineteenth century. Many promoters, as they planned turnpikes, and most states, as they chartered the new companies, were guided by the advice given in Albert Gallatin's 1808 plan for internal improvements. Gallatin urged the reduction of hills with few grades above three per cent, a sufficient crown in the road to provide good drainage, the economy of straight roads to reduce mileage, and the hard surfacing of any road that would be extensively used. He estimated that the costs of construction should range from $500 per mile for a dirt road with some hill reduction, to $7,000 a mile for a first-class hard-surfaced dual-lane road. Most state charters insisted on standards concerning construction, maximum grade, ditching, surfacing, and maintenance. Charters normally granted the turnpike company the right of eminent domain in route selection and the acquisition of construction materials. Often the charters also granted toll exemptions to certain classes of travelers. Commonly exempted were persons going to public worship or funerals, farmers on normal daily farm business, and militiamen on their way to a muster day. Most turnpikes were financed by private capital, but such states as Pennsylvania, Virginia, and Ohio invested substantial amounts of state funds in turnpike ventures. In South Carolina and Indiana modest amounts of money were spent on state-owned turnpikes.[11]

During the era of turnpikes New York State was first in total road mileage. Before the coming of the improved roads few travelers had many compliments for the state's public roads. Timothy Dwight, the president of Yale University and an ardent traveler, in 1799 found the public roads so wet and muddy that he and his companion had to walk their horses the last 30 miles into Utica. Five years later, near Buffalo, he found mud so deep that it "took three hours to cover a distance of four miles." The first turnpike in New York was the Albany and Schenectady Turnpike, a 14-mile road capitalized at

$140,000, which was chartered in 1797, reorganized in 1802, and completed in 1805. It was the first of seven turnpikes serving Albany and a portion of the major chain of several pikes running west toward Lake Erie. A majority of the first turnpikes in the state were either part of this east-west route or served towns along the Hudson River between New York City and Albany. By 1807 the New York legislature had given charters to sixty-seven different turnpikes with a total capital of more than $5 million and projected total routes of more than 3,000 miles. In 1807 only twenty-eight of the turnpikes were finished, with tolls being collected on about 900 miles of road.[12]

New York continued to project and build more improved roads. By 1812 a through route of connecting turnpikes ran from the Massachusetts state line to Lake Erie, a distance of well over 300 miles. In 1817, the year that New York started the Erie Canal, the state legislature chartered an additional twenty-four turnpike and bridge companies. By 1822 about $11 million of stock had been invested in 278 New York turnpikes with 6,000 miles of projected route and about 4,000 miles in active use. By 1830 the active number of turnpikes had declined to only 255. This decline was reflected in the action of the state legislature in its session of 1832. In that year only five new turnpikes were chartered, while twenty-five railroads were given acts of incorporation. An increase in wagon freighting at cheaper rates, more frequent stagecoach service, and the establishment of dozens and dozens of new inns accompanied the turnpike boom in New York. With the opening of the Erie Canal in 1825 most of the east-west freight traffic was lost by the wagoners, but many travelers still preferred the stagecoach to the packet boat. Stagecoaches were generally faster, continued to operate in winter months, and provided a greater variety of scenery. Timothy Dwight was not so happy with the inns along the roads of southeastern New York. Stopping at several that would not serve him dinner, he decided that many New York "inns" were in reality little more than "dramshops."[13]

The six states of New England together built slightly less toll-road mileage than that of New York. Many of the roads were chartered in the decade of 1797–1806, and by the latter year 135 companies had been established with total planned routes of more than 2,500 miles. Most of these roads were complete by 1812. By the end of the turnpike era in the 1830's, something over 300 different companies in the six states had invested more than $6 million in some 3,700 miles of improved road mileage.[14]

The great majority of the turnpikes of New England were located in the three southern states of Massachusetts, Connecticut, and Rhode Island. However, both Vermont and New Hampshire had several short roads as feeder lines to the Connecticut River or Lake Champlain. In the fall of 1812 Timothy Dwight found many of the New Hampshire roads "to a great extent excellent." Most New England companies emphasized the directness of route and the saving of mileage as they planned their new turnpikes. In 1803 Dwight noted that the new road from New Haven to Hartford was reported to deviate from a straight route by only 109 rods, saving about five miles over the old road. One result of the new direct routes was a reduction in the road mileage between Boston and New York City from 254 miles in 1806 to 210 miles in

1821. Many of the Massachusetts turnpikes, especially those serving Boston, were hard-surfaced. As a result, the average costs per mile in the Bay State were relatively high—in 1807 Albert Gallatin reported that many were costing $3,000 or more per mile. In contrast, the improved roads in Connecticut, which generally were not the all-weather type, cost much less. In 1807 thirty Connecticut turnpikes, with a total of 600 route miles, were being built for an average of well under $1,000 a mile. An acquaintance of Gallatin's reported that since Connecticut had few "great market towns," improved "roads of earth" were entirely satisfactory. Most of the forty turnpikes in Rhode Island were short, and many of them radiated out of Providence to different parts of the state. In the spring of 1825 Anne Royall, the liberal Washington journalist, took a stagecoach from Boston to Providence, for a steamboat connection to New York City, and the entire trip cost her $14.[15]

During the era of turnpikes Pennsylvania was easily the second state in mileage, just behind New York. In fact, New York, Pennsylvania, and the New England states together built well over 80 per cent of all the toll roads in the nation. The early success of the Philadelphia and Lancaster Turnpike was soon copied in Pennsylvania with such roads as the Susquehanna and Lehigh Turnpike and the Germantown and Perkiomen Turnpike. The 25-mile Germantown and Perkiomen was built between 1801 and 1804 for $285,000, an average of over $11,000 for each mile of the hard-surfaced all-weather route. In its first year of operation it received tolls of about $19,000, had expenses of about $10,000, and paid 3.5 per cent dividends. Many other turnpikes were soon chartered, most of them with certain legislative restrictions, a common one being a prohibition of any grades or ascents of more than five per cent.[16]

By 1821 about 150 different turnpikes had been chartered with a planned total route of 2,500 miles, of which 1,800 miles had been completed. More than two-thirds, 1,250 miles, of the completed mileage was built with stone. Of the $6,400,000 invested in the 150 companies, well over a third —$2,240,000—had come from the state. Pennsylvania was by far the most generous of the states in providing public funds for turnpike construction. The completed mileage in the state was up to 2,380 miles in 1828. By 1835 the total turnpike mileage was 2,500 miles and the state had chartered 220 turnpike companies. As the roads were built all across the state, wagon freight traffic greatly increased. In the month of March, 1830, the gatekeeper at the eastern gate of the Chambersburg Turnpike collected tolls on freight headed for Philadelphia and Baltimore that included: 3,450 barrels of flour, 364 barrels of whiskey, 134,000 pounds of bacon, 9,800 pounds of paper, 62,000 pounds of glass, 72,000 pounds of feathers. Even with such traffic, few of the improved roads in the state were bringing any profit to their owners. In the early summer of 1828 George W. Smith, a supporter of internal improvements, reported in Samuel Hazard's *Register of Pennsylvania* that "None of them [turnpikes] have yielded little more than has been expended in their repairs."[17]

In the remaining states of the Union turnpike building was less important. Since New Jersey had no cities of major commercial importance, fewer voices were raised in the state in sponsorship of improved roads. However, farmers did desire better markets for their crops and many people desired better and easier travel between New York City and Philadelphia. By 1829 about 550 miles of toll roads had been built in New Jersey, mostly in the northern and central parts of the state. In Maryland several turnpikes were projected, especially roads radiating from Baltimore. Even though Albert Gallatin had stressed the importance of the connecting road from Baltimore to the National Road at Cumberland, the completion of this route was much delayed. By 1830 Maryland had about 300 miles of turnpikes in operation. In the South there was considerable talk about the improvement of roads, but very little action. Two roads in Virginia were eventually finished and several short roads were built in South Carolina. West of Pennsylvania, except for the National Road, the most significant turnpike construction was in Ohio, but most of the new roads in that state were neither well constructed nor managed.[18]

In the first decades of the nineteenth century the turnpikes of the United States were crowded with a varied and colorful traffic. Heavy freight wagons slowly carried manufactured goods to western towns and returned with farm produce for seaport markets. The nearly endless stream of westward-moving emigrants met droves of cattle, hogs, sheep, and horses being driven to eastern markets in Baltimore, Philadelphia, or New York City. In faster motion were the brightly colored stagecoaches with their loads of passengers and mail.

Stagecoaches were certainly numerous on the turnpikes of the early nineteenth century. This was especially true on the routes of travel between major cities. Since many stage lines managed to get discount toll rates, turnpike revenue from

coaching companies was rarely large. In Pennsylvania many
stage lines paid only from a sixth to a half of the listed toll
rates.[19]

Stage travel grew rapidly in the first third of the century,
especially in the major eastern cities. Boston in 1801 was
served by some two dozen lines with a bit more than a hundred
arrivals and departures each week. By 1826 more than seventy-five separate lines operated out of Boston with a hundred
arrivals and departures daily. In 1826 the *American Traveller*
claimed: "Now there is scarce a town in New England through
which a stagecoach with elegant horses and careful attentive
drivers, does not pass, either once, twice, or thrice a week."
By 1832 it was estimated that the stage traffic between Boston
and Worcester was over 14,000 passengers a year. Albany
was nearly as important a center for stagecoach travel as
Boston, with more than a hundred arriving and departing
stages daily. Pennsylvania boosters claimed that between 1805
and 1834 the volume of stage travel between Philadelphia and
Pittsburgh had increased some thirtyfold. By 1819 some stage
service extended as far westward as Vincennes and St. Louis.[20]

The improved roads sped up the rate of travel. During the
turnpike era the scheduled time for stage travel between
Philadelphia and Pittsburgh was cut from a week to only
three days. Between 1800 and 1825 the best schedule of the
Boston to New York City stage dropped from seventy-four to
forty-one hours. In 1819 the Citizens Line of coaches often
made the New York to Philadelphia trip in eight and a half
hours or at a rate of more than 11 miles per hour. The stage
drivers often had good horses, and they naturally drove in a
grand manner, reserving their best speed for arrival at a

tavern stop or the entrance into town. Many veteran stagecoach patrons claimed the typical driver would never accept a tip but rarely refused a drink.[21]

Stage travel was not cheap and sometimes not too comfortable. At a time when a dollar a day in wages was excellent pay for most workers, paying from 4 to 6 cents a mile for stage travel was quite expensive. In 1825 a 167-mile trip from Albany to Boston cost $8.50, while a shorter 100-mile ride to Hartford was $4. In 1839 a stage ticket from Frederick, Maryland, to Wheeling, Virginia, was $9, while the 243-mile stage trip from Wheeling to Cincinnati was $18. If the road was muddy, the coach old, or the turnpike in poor repair, the ride could be tiring and irksome as well as expensive. George Sumner wrote of a trip into Pittsburgh:

> For two days and two nights was my body exposed to the thumps of this horrid road, and when I got to Pittsburgh (after having broken down twice, and got out three times during one night and broken down fence rails to pry the coach out of the mud) my body was a perfect jelly—without one sound spot upon it, too tired to stand, too sore to sit.

A Swedish visitor to America, Carl D. Arfwedson, had an even more dangerous experience in the early 1830's on a trip east of Cumberland when a dilapidated stagecoach started to fall apart:

> In the middle of a steep hill, down which the imprudent coachman drove a full gallop, both hind springs gave way. The shock which the body of the coach received from the lower part of the vehicle was so violent, that the bottom [of the coach] broke out, and before the travellers had had time to recover from their consternation, their feet were dangling through the opening. . . .

When the coach was finally stopped the driver exclaimed,

"What, in the name of God, has happened to the bottom?" [22]

But the stagecoaches, uncomfortable as they might be, had improved during the era of turnpikes. In the last years of the eighteenth century the coaches were generally awkward and clumsy. The passengers, entering at the front, had to climb over two or three fixed benches to gain a rear seat. Soon Levi Pease, a major stagecoach operator in Boston, designed a coach with a side door. It had a graceful oval shape and seated nine passengers in three rows of seats. By the late 1820's the best coaches were being built in Concord, New Hampshire, where Lewis Downing and Stephen Abbott, skilled Yankee wheelwrights, would eventually build hundreds of their famous Concord coaches. [23]

A by-product of improved roads and the expanded stage service was an increase in the frequency and speed of postal service. In 1789 there were only seventy-five post offices in the nation with about 2,400 miles of post roads. By 1830 the number of post offices had grown to 8,000 and some 115,000 miles of postal routes served the country. The increased use of stage-mail routes accompanied this great increase. By 1817 a mail coach was giving postal service over the 440-mile route from Pittsburgh to Louisville in seven days. In 1830 the *American Traveller* reported that the average mail contract with a mail coach was costing about 13 cents a mile. Thus the typical mail coach was obtaining probably a third of its revenue from the Post Office Department. [24]

While not as colorful as the stagecoach traffic, the wagon freight on the turnpikes was equally important, and generally produced more tollgate revenue. The volume of the wagon traffic was heavy. Thousands of wagons each year used the

National Road and other turnpike routes. A traveler west of
Baltimore in 1827 reported seeing 235 wagons in a distance
of only thirty-five miles. Many of the freight carriers were
Conestoga wagons, a ponderous vehicle that had been developed before the Revolution by the farmers of the Conestoga
Valley in eastern Pennsylvania. Such wagons rolled on heavy
wheels with wide tires, had a curved wagon bed to keep the
freight in place on steep grades, and a homespun hemp or
canvas stretched over curved hickory bows as a protection
against the weather. Pulled by four, six, or even eight hefty
horses, a Conestoga could carry fourteen barrels of flour over
the mountains of Pennsylvania. The drivers of these wagons
were a hardy and lusty group. Timothy Flint, a frontier mis-
sionary and preacher, described the Pennsylvania wagoners as
"A new species, perfectly unique in their language . . . more
rude profane and selfish than . . . boatsmen or hunters. . . .
We found them addicted to drunkenness and very little disposed to assist one another." Even so, many wagoners who
started out as young drivers at $8 to $10 a month after a few
years of hard labor were the owners of a dozen or more teams
and wagons. The wagon traffic on some routes was so heavy
that a number of taverns were operated exclusively for the
drivers. Such taverns might house as many as forty to fifty
wagoners with their teams each night. What the innkeepers
might lose in inexpensive morning and evening meals was generally more than regained in the heavy sale of whiskey and the
free manure left in the yard.[25]
    Wagon freight was not cheap. Early in the nineteenth cen-
tury John Melish reported that wagon freight between Philadelphia and Pittsburgh was costing about $5 per hundred

pounds. For the first three decades of the century average wagon rates ranged from 30 to 70 cents per ton-mile. Even at these high rates *Niles' Weekly Register* in 1823 reported that few farmers could successfully compete, with their own teams and wagons, against the rates offered by the wagoners. The total volume moved was substantial. In the eight months, April 1 to December 1, 1815, the freight moving by wagon in and out of Pittsburgh was estimated to have a value of just under $4 million and to have paid freight rates of more than $350,000. Wagon freight was not fast. A thirteen-day trip for the 290 miles from Philadelphia to Pittsburgh was about normal, and the Conestoga that covered the 90 miles from New York to Philadelphia in three days was called the "flying machine." When canals began to appear in the 1820's and 1830's they provided cheaper and sometimes faster freight movement. But some merchants continued to favor wagon freight because of the convenience of door-to-door service. The canal network at its height never came close to the more extensive network of turnpikes and common roads. Also, highway transport was available during much of the winter when canals were frozen shut. Not all the wagons on the turnpikes were carrying freight. Many were carrying settlers moving west. The Englishman Henry B. Fearon, while traveling by stage across Pennsylvania in the fall of 1817, overtook 103 freight wagons headed west for Pittsburgh. In the same two and a half days his coach overtook 63 emigrant wagons headed for new homes in the West. More than two-thirds of the wagons were from New England.[26]

Although the turnpikes were crowded with traffic, financially most of them were disappointments to the investors and promoters who built them. From the 1820's on, an increasingly rapid decline in both the construction and use of turnpikes in America occurred for a variety of reasons. In the 1820's and after, new transportation facilities — the steamboat, the canal, the railroad — increasingly challenged the turnpike. Canal freight rates were cheap, and the average canal boat could carry ten times the load of a four-horse Conestoga wagon. Near the Old Post Road in New England, sometimes an upstart village not on a turnpike would successfully bid for a stop on a projected railroad. Once the town had obtained the steamcars with all its new passenger traffic, the older "turnpike village" was left to decay along with its empty stables and languishing stage taverns. Sometimes the better stagecoaches were sent to western states to serve a frontier region without any railroad service.

Toll revenues rarely came up to expectations. The problem was compounded by the presence of "shunpikes" — short routes around tollgates that were used by dishonest teamsters and drivers. Finding honest tollgate keepers was so difficult that some companies sold the right to operate the gates for a fixed sum. In Pennsylvania the editor Samuel Hazard wrote of the turnpikes in his state: "None of them have yielded dividends sufficient to remunerate the proprietors, most of them have yielded little more than has been expended in their repairs; and some have yielded tolls not sufficient even for this purpose." Turnpike dividends in the rest of the nation were no more plentiful. Even in New England, where the most successful turnpikes were located, few returned a real profit. Albert Gallatin reported that in Connecticut newly built turnpikes often had to spend more than half their toll revenue for road repairs. With the appearance of canals and later the railroads, more and more turnpike companies sought to abandon their roads and return them to free public use. By 1835 half the turnpikes in Massachusetts had been partially or totally given up. In the same years about half of the New York turnpike network was abandoned. The process of abandonment was somewhat slower in Maryland and Pennsylvania. In the Keystone State thirteen turnpike companies in the spring of 1833 decided to ask the state legislature to appropriate money to help them get out of debt.[27]

A major portion of the decline of turnpikes was caused by certain deficiencies within the turnpike system itself, and thus appeared before the completion of many canals. Although the era of turnpikes in the first decades of the nineteenth century was generally a financial failure, many different groups benefited from the thousands of miles of new and improved roads. Certainly a new national unity had grown out of the easier communications and travel which had come with the turnpike.

Water transport, both by river and along the coast, had been of prime importance to Americans throughout the entire colonial period. As settlement pushed into the interior, river traffic became more and more important from Maine to Georgia. In 1818 *Niles' Weekly Register* claimed that in South Carolina two-thirds of all marketable farm crops were raised within five miles of a river.[28]

In New England successful canals were becoming common before the American Revolution, and soon some Americans were endorsing and planning the building of man-made water-

ways. As early as 1772 Benjamin Franklin, then in England,
had written an endorsement of canals to the mayor of Philadelphia: "I am glad my Canal Papers were agreeable to you.
. . . Rivers are ungovernable things, especially in hilly countries. Canals are quiet and very manageable." Unfortunately,
Franklin's early efforts to help Philadelphia build a canal
were not successful. Shortly after his retirement to Mount
Vernon in 1783, George Washington became interested in improving navigation on the Potomac River. In 1785 both Maryland and Virginia chartered the Potomac Company, which
was charged with building short canals around the Potomac
Rapids north of Georgetown, Maryland. Washington was
made president of the company, and with $200,000 of sub-
scribed capital five short canals were completed between
Georgetown and Harper's Ferry. Washington also headed the
James River and Kanawha Company, which eventually dug
two short canals around the falls of the James River above
Richmond.[29]

Farther south two other canals were dug during the last
years of the century. Between 1787 and 1794 the Dismal
Swamp Canal was sponsored and built by Virginia and North
Carolina to provide a connecting water link between Norfolk
and Albemarle Sound to the south. The Santee and Cooper
Canal, connecting those two rivers, was a 22-mile canal completed in 1802 to provide a better route for the cotton, rice,
and indigo of South Carolina to reach the Charleston market.
In New England the principal early waterway was the Middlesex Canal, chartered in 1793 by Massachusetts to direct the
inland trade of the Merrimack River toward Boston. The 28-
mile canal, including twenty locks, took ten years to build and

cost $554,000. Thus in the thirty years between Washington's first canal-building efforts and the Treaty of Ghent, the canal era had barely begun. Many man-made waterways had been projected, but relatively few built. In 1816 little more than a hundred miles of canal had been completed in the entire nation. It seemed that many Americans agreed with Thomas Jefferson, who, when asked in 1809 to endorse the projected Erie Canal, was reported to have said: "It is a noble project, but you are a century too soon." [30]

In spite of Jefferson's pessimism, the idea of connecting the waters of the upper Hudson River with those of Lake Erie dated back to the era of the Revolution. In 1774 Colonial Governor William Tryon of New York had recommended a system of locks and canals to aid navigation in the Mohawk and upper Hudson valleys. A longer canal to the inland lakes had been suggested by Gouverneur Morris in 1777. After the Revolution, a company to build locks and short canals around portions of the Mohawk was organized, with General Philip Schuyler as president, but the company did not prosper. Later, Albert Gallatin included an east-west canal across New York State in his plan for internal improvements. [31]

Vigorous action in support of the Erie Canal came only after the War of 1812. Several New Yorkers were eager to sponsor a canal to Lake Erie in the middle teens, but chief among them was DeWitt Clinton, long-time mayor of New York City. Clinton was an energetic mayor who was interested in public education, hospitals, and orphan asylums as well as the construction of the Erie Canal. He was a member of a seven-man committee charged with submitting a canal plan for the state. This group proposed a 364-mile canal to extend from Albany to Buffalo on Lake Erie. Shortly after Clinton was elected governor of New York, the two houses of the state legislature, in April, 1817, approved the committee's plans. In the same session the legislature approved the construction of the Champlain Canal connecting the lake with the upper Hudson. Other laws passed chartered two dozen turnpike and bridge companies, as well as several banks and a new county. But the big news was the approval of the Erie Canal, by far the biggest project of its kind in America.[32]

The digging of the Erie started at the little wilderness village of Rome, New York, on July 4, 1817. From this time on, Independence Day was to be the favorite time for the official sod-breaking of nearly all subsequent canals. Rome had been selected as the starting place because it was a midpoint, where work could proceed through level terrain in both directions at once. After speeches by assorted notables, the first earth was turned by Judge John Richardson, one of the first men to take up a construction contract on the canal. Cannons boomed and the crowd cheered as work was thus started on "Clinton's Big Ditch."[33]

The Erie Canal was to be forty feet wide at the surface and twenty-eight feet in width at the bottom, with a water depth of four feet. Along one side a towpath would be built for horses and mules to pull the canal boats. Fortunately, there were no major hills or mountains to cross, but there was a total drop of 565 feet between the level of Lake Erie and the Hudson River at Albany. Near Syracuse and also near the Montezuma Marshes there were broad valleys to cross. Thus, counting all the steps up and down across the state, a canal boat would travel a vertical distance of 675 feet. Eighty-three locks, with

lifts varying from six to twelve feet, were built to take care of
the several necessary ascents and descents. Eighteeen aqueducts were also built for the crossing of creeks and rivers.[34]

The canal commissioners had few qualified engineers to
help them face the engineering problem of such an immense
project. Instead, they turned to two country lawyers, Benjamin
Wright and James Geddes, both of whom had earlier engaged
in surveying work. The two canal "engineers" amazed and
silenced their critics when their individual canal surveys, covering a distance of more than a hundred miles, came together
with a level difference of less than one and a half inches. One
of Wright's assistants, Canvass White, was sent to England to
observe methods of canal building there, especially the use of
underwater cement. Upon his return, White experimented
with varieties of New York limestone, and soon developed a
quicklime cement which easily hardened under water. This
new hydraulic cement was very useful in the construction of
locks, and more than 400,000 bushels were used on the Erie
Canal. Other valuable engineers on the project were Nathan S.
Roberts, who designed the five double combined locks used at
Lockport, and John B. Jervis, who later shifted to building
railroads. Most of the actual excavation was done by small
contractors, often well-to-do local farmers, who agreed to dig
a short length of canal for a fixed price. Their workers were
native New Yorkers or recent immigrants from Ireland, who
were paid 50 to 80 cents a day plus rations of food and whiskey. At first their tools were axes, spades, picks, and wheel-
barrows, but before long these were being supplemented with
horse-drawn plows, scrapers, carts, and huge circular "stump
pullers."[35]

Construction progress was slow but steady. In the fall of 1819 the canal commissioners navigated the canal from Utica to Rome, and by 1822 about 220 miles of waterway were in use. Buffalo merchants were soon claiming that the partially opened canal had already reduced the freight charges on merchandise from New York City to the relatively low figure of $37.50 per ton. As each new section was opened traffic crowded in, and the collected tolls helped finance and hasten the completion of the project. By the spring of 1825 the canal was nearly completed, and as Lafayette finished his grand tour of America, he traveled much of the distance from Buffalo to Albany via the new waterway. The celebration of the completion of the great project started on October 26, 1825, when five canal boats left Buffalo for Albany and New York City. On board the lead boat, the *Seneca Chief*, were Governor Clinton, a band of beaver-hatted dignitaries, and two brightly painted kegs filled with water from Lake Erie. The flotilla of boats grew in number as it moved across the state. The happy and excited citizens of the canal towns tried to outdo each other with pageants, celebrations, banquets, and numerous lighted transparencies. The long string of boats reached Albany on November 2 and New York City two days later. Surrounded by hundreds of boats, the *Seneca Chief* finally reached lower New York Harbor, where Clinton performed the wedding of the waters by emptying a keg of Lake Erie water into the ocean. After eight years of hard labor, and the expenditure of nearly $8 million, the Erie Canal was open.[36]

The success of the Erie was immediate. Yearly tolls collected were up to nearly $700,000 in 1826, and before long were well over a million dollars. Within little more than a

decade the toll revenue had paid for the canal. Shortly after
the completion of the Erie, Jefferson was reported to have
admitted to DeWitt Clinton: "I now perceive, that, in regard
to your resources and energies, I committed an error of a
century in my calculation." Yearly canal boat traffic near
Schenectady climbed from 6,000 boats in 1824 to 15,000 in
1826, and 23,000 by 1834. As the traffic increased, there was
talk of enlargement, and in 1835, only ten years after its completion, the state of New York decided to enlarge the canal.[37]

The Erie's success created a canal-building craze that
spread from New England to Virginia and westward to Illinois. Soon dozens of projected canals were planned, all hop-
ing to match the profitability of the New York waterway.
Canals were much larger projects than the earlier turnpikes.
Turnpikes were generally not very long, and at a cost as low
as several hundred dollars a mile often represented a total
investment of no more than ten to fifty thousand dollars.
Canals represented larger investments, generally in the millions of dollars—the Erie cost nearly $22,000 a mile, while
the Chesapeake and Ohio Canal cost about $60,000 a mile.
Since such huge investments were normally beyond the reach
of private capital, most canals were built and financed with
public funds, generally being owned by state governments.
The federal government had given no aid in building the Erie,
but later it did grant about 4 million acres of the public domain to aid canal projects in several western states.[38]

The canal-building craze was at its peak between 1825, the
year the Erie was completed, and 1840. By 1830 some 1,200
miles of canals had been built in thirteen states, and a decade
later 3,300 miles were in operation in twenty states. Although

building slowed during the forties, nearly 3,700 miles were in operation by 1850. In that year only six states east of the Mississippi had no canals, and eight states had a hundred miles or more of the man-made waterways. At midcentury Pennsylvania had the greatest mileage (954 miles), New York was second with 803 miles, and Ohio, with 792 miles, was third. Most of the canals built in these years were of three types: 1) those, like the Erie, built to connect the Atlantic states with Lake Erie or the valley of the Ohio River; 2) those to improve transportation between up-country and tidewater in the Atlantic states; 3) those in the West which sought to connect the Great Lakes with the Ohio River.[39]

As the Erie was being completed, the merchants of Philadelphia became fearful that their western trade might be lost to the Empire State. Despite opposition, canal boosters in Pennsylvania prevailed, and on July 4, 1826, the first spadeful of earth was turned on the middle section of the Grand Canal, running from the Susquehanna to Hollidaysburg. East of the Susquehanna a completed canal, and later a railroad, gave service to Philadelphia. The 35-mile Portage Railroad, consisting of several inclined planes, was built to haul the canal boats over the crest of the Appalachians between Hollidaysburg and Johnstown. West of Johnstown a second canal was built on to Pittsburgh. By 1834 the entire 395-mile Pennsylvania Main Line, consisting of a railway, canals, and inclined planes, was completed at a cost of more than $10 million. This second waterway to western markets had considerable traffic but it never became a serious rival of the Erie. The Pennsylvania canal had been built to the same general specifications as the Erie, and much of its construction was directed by the Erie veterans James Geddes and Nathan Roberts. But the Appalachians are steep, and the Pennsylvania route rose 2,200 feet above sea level, as compared to the maximum altitude on the Erie of 650 feet. The 174 locks on the Pennsylvania canal were more than double the number on the Erie, and the inclined planes proved to be a serious bottleneck. Toll revenue never matched that of the Erie, and the total revenue on the Pennsylvania system between 1829 and 1840 did not quite equal the repair and maintenance costs. The Main Line never paid its way, and portions of the route were later sold to the Pennsylvania Railroad.[40]

During the same years, two other efforts were made to cross the mountains with canals, one in Maryland and one in Virginia. Washington's dream of a waterway over the mountains seemed closer to reality when President John Quincy Adams, using a ribbon-bedecked spade, started the new Chesapeake and Ohio Canal at Georgetown on July 4, 1828. The first time the President's spade dug into the earth he struck a root. He tried a second and third time before getting a full shovelful of dirt. Later, in his diary, Adams admitted that the incident of the tree root ". . . struck the eye and fancy of the spectators more than all the flowers of rhetoric in my speech. . . ." Work on the C. & O. canal never did get into high gear. Sickness and labor problems plagued the company. The Blue Ridge mountains were also a handicap. Eleven million dollars had been spent, but when digging finally stopped in 1850 the canal was finished only 184 miles to Cumberland. A second canal, the James River and Kanawha in Virginia, was no more of a success. Midcentury found work on that canal stalled on the upper James River at Buchanan, not quite 200 miles above

Richmond.[41]

Both New York and Pennsylvania also built several shorter branch canals tributary to the Erie or the Pennsylvania Main Line. The Pennsylvania system of canals connected with those of New York on the upper Susquehanna west of Binghamton, and with those of Ohio northwest of Pittsburgh. New England never really joined the craze for canals, and less than 200 miles were built in the six-state area.

Perhaps the most important of the shorter canals in the middle Atlantic states were the tidewater canals which carried coal to Philadelphia and New York City markets. These "anthracite canals," most of which were privately owned, were generally financially successful. The most northern of the coal canals was the Delaware and Hudson, running from Honesdale, Pennsylvania to the Delaware River and continuing in a northeasterly direction across New York to Kingston on the Hudson River. Finished in 1828 under the direction of John B. Jervis, the 106-mile canal eventually paid good dividends in the 1840's and 1850's. Farther south, the 48-mile Lehigh Canal, from White Haven, Pennsylvania, to Easton on the Delaware, connected with the Morris Canal, which wound 102 miles through northern New Jersey before reaching Newark Bay. The Lehigh was a profitable venture but the poorly managed Morris Canal was never as successful. Other coal-bearing canals were the Pennsylvania-owned 60-mile Delaware Division Canal, which paralleled the Delaware upriver from Philadelphia, and the 60-mile Delaware and Raritan Canal, running from Trenton across New Jersey to tidewater at New Brunswick.[42]

In the West the great bulk of canal building was located in

the states of Ohio, Indiana, and Illinois. Even before the Erie Canal was completed the Ohio legislature was planning its own extensive system of canals. On July 4, 1825, DeWitt Clinton left New York long enough to help break ground on the state-sponsored Ohio and Erie Canal, a 308-mile route from Cleveland to Portsmouth on the Ohio River. Later, several branches were added, providing canal service to Columbus, a connection with the Pennsylvania system, and a second route to the Ohio River. A second north-south waterway across Ohio, the Miami and Erie, a 244-mile canal from Toledo, via Dayton, to Cincinnati on the Ohio, was also started in 1825. For a short time James Geddes helped with the planning of the Ohio canal system, but the major driving force behind the canals in the Buckeye State was Alfred Kelley. Kelley was so greatly enthused with the "canal fever" that he gave up a profitable Cleveland law practice to become the Ohio canal commissioner. At a total cost of $8 million the Ohio and Erie Canal was completed in 1833, but the Miami and Erie was not finished until 1845. Although neither canal ever fully paid for itself, Ohio's canal system did open up rich markets for the farms and towns of the state.[43]

Indiana had a desire for canals just as great as that of Ohio. Helped by an 1827 land grant from the federal government, Indiana planned the Wabash and Erie Canal to connect the upper Wabash River with Ohio's Miami and Erie Canal. Started in 1832, the construction of the Wabash and Erie was aided by Indiana's Internal Improvement Bill of 1836. Progress was still slow, but the canal reached Lafayette by 1843, and was extended on to Evansville on the Ohio River by 1853. A shorter canal, the White Water, allowed farmers in southeastern Indiana to move their crops to the Ohio River. Both canals received tolls only sufficient to pay for minimum repairs, thus leaving the state with a crushing internal improvement debt of $13 million. In Illinois a more successful venture was the Illinois and Michigan Canal, which connected LaSalle, on the upper Illinois River, with Lake Michigan at Chicago. When this canal was completed in 1848 the heavy freight traffic soon helped change the frontier town of Chicago into a booming commercial city.[44]

American canals, whether or not they were producing a profit, were crowded with both freight and passenger traffic in the generation after the building of the Erie. This was true of the canals of New York, Pennsylvania, Maryland, and the western states. Packets filled with passengers, lineboats carrying emigrants moving west, and the still-slower freighters all crowded the canals. The traffic on the Erie was probably typical. In 1838 the total Erie tolls received were $1,590,000 paid for hundreds of packet passages, plus assorted freight weighing one and a third million tons valued at about $65,000,000. About a seventh of the tolls were paid for passenger travel, a seventh for forest products, nearly 30 per cent for farm produce, and nearly 40 per cent for merchandise and manufactured goods.[45]

The finest boats on the canals naturally were the passenger-carrying packets. The average packet was sixty to seventy feet in length by fifteen feet in width, cost from $1,000 to $1,500 to build, and was the ultimate in luxury and speed. When entering locks or passing, a packet normally had the right of way over freighters and other craft. It was pulled by the best horses and could cover a hundred miles in 24 hours. For all this speed and service the passenger paid 4 to 5 cents a mile. The fare included meals which were generally abundant and sometimes of first quality. The competition among packet lines was keen, especially on the Erie, and not all the packet owners found their service to be profitable.[46]

At one end of the long packet cabin was the kitchen and crew quarters. The remaining area, often called the "Saloon," served both for dining and sleeping. At night, sleeping quarters for the women was partitioned off with a curtain, and became, as the Swedish traveler Carl Arfwedson described it, "A sanctuary into which the profane dared not set foot." Such a sanctuary did not satisfy Mrs. Frances Trollope, an English visitor rarely enthusiastic about America. After a trip on the Erie, she wrote: "I can hardly imagine any motive . . . powerful enough to induce me to again imprison myself in a canal boat. . . ." After the ladies were settled, the more numerous male passengers drew lots for their berths, little five-and-a-half-foot by two-foot beds hanging three or four tiers deep along each side wall. When Charles Dickens first saw such sleeping arrangements, he was reminded of tightly packed horizontal bookshelves. Dickens was unlucky enough to draw a bottom "shelf" and finally managed to get to bed by rolling himself from the cabin floor onto the thin mattress. When Carl Arfwedson, also drawing a bottom berth, discovered that his two upper-berth mates were corpulent, he considered spending the night on the open deck above.[47]

Less impressive than packets were lineboats or emigrant boats, freighters, cabin and shanty boats, and finally the oxen-drawn lumber rafts. Thousands of crewmen—captains, steersmen, deckhands, and drivers—were needed to run the canal boats. Probably 25,000 were employed on the Erie alone. No crew member came close to a packet captain in status and self-esteem. In 1839 the visiting English naval officer Captain Frederick Marryat wrote: "An American packet captain is in his own opinion no small affair, he puffs and swells until he looks larger than his boat.[48]

On most canals the freighter was the craft most frequently seen. These stubby cargo carriers took on no passengers, but they carried mountains of freight. By 1850 the total freight moving east and west through the Erie was over 3 million tons. Boats moving east carried timber, livestock, furs, whiskey, cider, flour, and grain. Those returning west to Buffalo carried the assorted products of eastern factories: hardware, notions, bolts of calico, furniture, clocks, shoes, whalebone corsets. From the beginning, the freight costs by canal were several times cheaper than land haulage via turnpike. Canal tolls and freighter rates both continued to fall during the 1830's and 1840's, and by midcentury much of the freight passing through the Erie was moving at a penny a ton-mile or less.[49]

Canals went into decline with the coming of the railroad. In 1830 canal mileage was perhaps forty times that of the railroad. By 1840 canal and rail mileage was nearly equal, both about 3,300 miles. In 1850 rail mileage was two and a half times that of canal, and by 1860 the rail network of 30,000 miles was about ten times the canal mileage. During the 1850's the rail freight rates were two or three times those of the canal, but even so, the railroads of New York State were making gains at the expense of the Erie Canal. Between 1853 and 1859 freight ton-mileage increased greatly on the Erie Railroad and tripled on the New York Central. On the Erie

Canal in the same years it declined more than 20 per cent. The losses in Erie traffic were chiefly in the western movement of manufactured products.[50]

Railroads had two great advantages over canals: speed and location. Even the first railroads were several times faster than the best canal boats. The fastest time on Pennsylvania's Grand Canal system for a trip between Philadelphia and Pittsburgh was four and a half days; the new Pennsylvania Railroad soon was covering the distances in seventeen hours. Canals were stymied by hills of any size. They were built where geography favored them rather than where man wanted them. Most hills, and many mountains, could be crossed by a railroad if a civil engineer was given the task of surveying and laying out a modest gradient.

A major flaw in canal operation was the fact that it was closed from three to five months a year because of cold weather. During the twenty-six years 1824 through 1849 the Erie, on average, was open 232 days a year and closed 133 days. Its opening dates ranged from March 27 to May 2, and its closing dates from November 23 to December 21. Canals in Pennsylvania, Maryland, and Virginia might be open a few weeks longer, but none could offer the year-round service of the railroad. Many canals had other problems not foreseen by their promoters. Expenses for repairs were generally larger than expected. Flooding was very troublesome for some canals. Needed repairs and flooding problems sometimes caused canals to be closed even in mid-season. Locks frequently restricted traffic more than original estimates had suggested. In the end, few canals, except for the Erie and several anthracite canals, ever returned a profit to their owners.[51]

In the half-century before the Civil War many new modes of transport appeared in turn. Turnpike, Conestoga wagon, and Concord coach gave way to canal boat and packet, to be supplemented in turn by stern-wheeler and side-wheeler on almost every river in the country. Before the typical turnpike had started to return its original investment—almost before the memory of the toasts and illuminated banners used to celebrate the opening of the Erie Canal had faded, and long before the first federal safety regulation for river steamboats (1838)—another challenger appeared in the form of the flanged wheel, iron rail, and puffing locomotive. Perhaps the most significant theme in the early transportation history of this country was the tendency of each new type to be so quickly challenged by the succeeding type that no single mode of transport had a decent interval in which to grow and prove itself.

But canals, like turnpikes, contributed much to America. Canals helped hundreds of thousands of people to move to new western homes. Farm produce that could never have been moved economically by wagon and turnpike could profitably go to market by canal boat. Factories boomed and small towns became prosperous cities as hundreds of packets and freighters were drawn along the placid canal waters. The canal era contributed much to the transportation revolution of the early nineteenth century, a revolution that was to help forge America into a rich industrial nation.

1. George R. Taylor, *The Transportation Revolution, 1815-1860* (New York, 1951), 18–19; *Annals of Congress*, 14th Congress, 2nd Ses., 853.
2. Joseph A. Durrenberger, *Turnpikes: A Study of the Toll Road Movement in the Middle Atlantic States and Maryland* (Valdosta, Ga., 1931), 45–75; Edward C. Kirkland, *Men, Cities and Transportation: A Study in New England Transportation, 1820-1900* (Cambridge, Mass., 1948), 50–51; Taylor, *Transportation Revolution*, 22, 32, 33.
3. *Ibid.*, 22–24, 79.
4. J. L. Ringwalt, *Development of Transportation Systems in the United States* (Philadelphia, 1888), 23; W. E. Lunt, *History of England* (New York, 1938), 584.
5. Christopher Colles, *A Survey of the Roads of the United States of America, 1789*, Walter W. Ristow, ed., (Cambridge, Mass., 1961), 96–106; Isaac Weld, Jr., *Travels Through the States of North America and the Provinces of Upper and Lower Canada, During the Years 1795, 1796, and 1797* (London, 1807), 1, 37–38.
6. Durrenberger, *Turnpikes*, 33.
7. *American State Papers, Miscellaneous* [Gallatin's Report], I, 863–65, 896; Durrenberger, *Turnpikes*, 52.
8. Francis Baily, *Journal of a Tour in Unsettled Parts of North America, 1796–1797* (London, 1856), 107; *American State Papers, Miscellaneous*, I, 893, 896.
9. Frederic L. Paxson, *History of the American Frontier,1763–1892* (Boston, 1924), 151–53; John Melish, *Information and Advice to Emigrants to the United States* (Philadelphia, 1819), 112; *Niles' Weekly Register*, XXII, 177.
10. *Ibid.*, XXI, 177, XXIII, 296, 303, 403; *Executive Document of the House of Representatives*, No. 76, Doc. 16, 17th Congress, 1st Ses. (1822).
11. *Niles' Weekly Register*, XV, 10–44; *American State Papers, Miscellaneous*, I, 742; Durrenberger, *Turnpikes*, 111; Taylor, *Transportation Revolution*, 24–26.
12. Timothy Dwight, *Travels in New England and New York, 1796–1815* (London, 1823), III, 124, IV, 35; Benjamin DeWitt, "A Sketch of the Turnpike Roads in the State of New York," *Trans-*

actions of the Society for the Promotion of Useful Arts in the State of New York (Albany, N.Y., 1807), II, 180–204.

13. Niles' Weekly Register, XII, 142; Sterling Goodenow, A Brief Topographical and Statistical Manual of the State of New York (New York, 1822), 17; Edwin Williams, New York Register for 1830 (New York, 1830), 179; American Annual Register (1831–32), VII, 249; Oliver W. Holmes, "The Turnpike Era," in Alexander C. Flick, ed., History of the State of New York (New York, 1933–37), V, 257–94; Dwight, Travels, IV, 11.

14. Kirkland, Men, Cities and Transportation, I, 32–48; Taylor, Transportation Revolution, 22–23.

15. Dwight, Travels IV, 98, II, 196; American Traveller (Boston), II, May 25, 1827; American State Papers, Miscellaneous I, 866–67, 870–72; Anne Royall, Sketches of History, Life and Manners in the United States (1826), 365.

16. American State Papers, Miscellaneous, I, 891–92; 883–84; Thomas F. Gordon, A Gazetteer of the State of Pennsylvania, (Philadelphia, 1832), 891–92.

17. American Annual Register, II, 469; Niles' Weekly Register, XXIII, 297; Samuel Hazard, The Register of Pennsylvania, I, 407, XVI, 90, V, 336, I, 407.

18. Durrenberger, Turnpikes, 65–75; American State Papers, Miscellaneous, I, 908–09; Taylor, Transportation Revolution, 25–26.

19. Durrenberger, Turnpikes, 121–22.

20. American Traveller, II, Nov. 7, 1826, Sept. 8, 1826, VII, Apr. 10, 1832; Williams, New York Register for 1830, 115; Hazard, Register of Pennsylvania, XIII, 384; Niles' Weekly Register, XVI, 256.

21. Durrenberger, Turnpikes, 127; Taylor, Transportation Revolution, 142; Niles' Weekly Register, XVI, 176; Robert E. Riegel, Young America, 1830–1840 (Norman, Okla., 1949), 152–53.

22. American Traveller, I, Sept. 6, 1825; Hazard's United States Commercial and Statistical Register, I, Nov. 13, 1839, 331; Riegel, Young America, 151; Carl D. Arfwedson, The United States and Canada in 1832, 1833, and 1834 (1834), II, 145–46.

23. Steward H. Holbrook, The Old Post Road (New York, 1962), 42–48.

24. *Niles' Weekly Register*, XII, 304; *American Traveller*, VI, Dec. 17, 1830.
25. Hazard, *Register of Pennsylvania*, XII, 286; Durrenberger, *Turnpikes*, 118–19.
26. John Melish, *Travels Through the United States* (Philadelphia, 1818), II, 313; Taylor, *Transportation Revolution*, 133; *Niles' Weekly Register*, XXIII, 296, X, 371, 231; Hazard, *Register of Pennsylvania*, VIII, 304; Henry B. Fearon, *Sketches of America* (London, 1819), 196.
27. Taylor, *Transportation Revolution*, 26–28; *American State Papers, Miscellaneous*, I, 871–72; Hazard, *Register of Pennsylvania*, I, 407, XII, 136, 286.
28. *Niles' Weekly Register*, XV, 135.
29. Ringwalt, *Development of Transportation Systems*, 41–42; Taylor, *Transportation Revolution*, 42–43.
30. *Ibid.*, 32; *Niles' Weekly Register*, XXXVII, 426; Madeline S. Waggoner, *The Long Haul West: The Great Canal Era, 1817–1850* (New York, 1958), 49.
31. Caroline E. MacGill, et. al., *History of Transportation in the United States before 1860* (Washington, D.C., 1917), 170–76; *Niles' Weekly Register*, XV, 10–12.
32. Taylor, *Transportation Revolution*, 32–33; *Niles' Weekly Register*, XII, 142.
33. Ronald E. Shaw, *Erie Water West: A History of the Erie Canal, 1792–1854* (Lexington, Ky., 1966), 84–85; *Niles' Weekly Register*, XII, 340.
34. Shaw, *Erie Water West*, 87.
35. *Ibid.*, 87–95; Taylor, *Transportation Revolution*, 34.
36. MacGill, *History of Transportation before 1860*, 189; *Niles' Weekly Register*, XX, 415; Taylor, *Transportation Revolution*, 34; Shaw, *Erie Water West*, 181–94.
37. *Ibid.*, 299; *Hazard's United States Commercial and Statistical Register*, I, 52; *Niles' Weekly Register*, XXXVII, 426.
38. Taylor, *Transportation Revolution*, 48–49.
39. *Ibid.*, 79, 37.
40. *Ibid.*, 43–45; *Hazard's United States Commercial and Statistical Register*, II, 35, IV, 268–69; Waggoner, *Long Haul West*, 191–203.

41. *Ibid.*, 294; Taylor, *Transportation Revolution*, 42–43; *Memoirs of John Quincy Adams* (Philadelphia, 1876), VIII, 49–50.
42. Taylor, *Transportation Revolution*, 38–41.
43. *Niles' Weekly Register*, XXVIII, 346; MacGill, *History of Transportation before 1860*, 287–90; Harry N. Scheiber, *Ohio Canal Era: A Case Study of Government and the Economy, 1820–1861* (Athens, Ohio, 1969), 17–23.
44. Taylor, *Transportation Revolution*, 47–48.
45. *Hazard's United States Commercial and Statistical Register*, I, 50, II, 248.
46. Theodore Dwight, *The Northern Traveller and Northern Tour* (New York, 1830), 47–48; *American Traveller*, I, Jan. 13, 1826.
47. Arfwedson, *United States and Canada*, II, 277–79; Frances Trollope, *Domestic Manners of the Americans* (New York, 1949), 369; Waggoner, *Long Haul West*, 150–53.
48. *Ibid.*, 135–37, 151.
49. Hazard, *Register of Pennsylvania* IV, 288, VII, 333; Williams, *New York Register for 1837*, 206; Taylor, *Transportation Revolution*, 137.
50. *American Railroad Journal*, May 12, 1860, 404; S. P. Chase, *Foreign and Domestic Commerce of the United States*, Senate Document 55, 38th Congress, 1st Ses., 1864, 133, 135, 181.
51. Joel Munsell, *Albany Annual Register for 1850*, 329.

The Building of the New York Central: A Study in the Development of the International Iron Trade

Ann M. Scanlon

During the 1830's, when the lines that made up the original New York Central Railroad were under construction, there were no manufacturing plants in the United States capable of rolling a single foot of iron rail. All rails, at this time, had to be imported from Great Britain. There were no facilities in the United States for their production until 1844.[1] American capitalists who were interested in building iron mills found it impossible to compete with their more technologically advanced rivals. In 1832 Welsh ironmasters could deliver flat rails in Boston, with all shipping and tariff duties paid, for $64 per ton. American manufacturers could not hope to supply the same rail for less than $125 per ton.[2] That same year, Congress eliminated the duty on railroad iron that was laid down within three years of importation.[3] This only served to further increase the difference between the price of American rails and those produced abroad.

The first locomotives used on American railroads were also made in Great Britain. But within a few years, American builders developed an exceptionally strong, lightweight engine that weighed only six to nine tons and employed a minimum amount of complicated machinery. Very few British locomotives were imported into the United States after 1840.[4] The Mohawk & Hudson, the first unit to be built in the future Central system, used both English and American models. In 1831 the company purchased the *John Bull* from the Robert Stevenson works at Newcastle-on-Tyne and the *DeWitt Clinton* from the West Point Foundry of Cold Spring, New York. About two years later, it purchased three additional locomotives, one from Rogers, Ketchum & Grosvenor of Paterson, New Jersey, and two from England.[5] The lines west of Schenectady purchased all their locomotives in the United States. Most of them came from Rogers, Ketchum & Grosvenor or Matthew Baldwin of Philadelphia or the West Point Foundry in New York City.[6]

The railroad companies consumed enormous quantities of iron. Their needs were not confined to single item or one-time purchases. The original track on most early lines consisted of flat, wrought iron strips secured by iron spikes to underlying wooden or stone stringers and reinforced at the joints with iron plates. Since the average life of flat rail was only eight or nine years, frequent replacement was necessary.[7]

By the mid-1840's most railroads began to replace their lightweight (15-21 tons per mile) flat rail with solid, wrought iron rail. The flat rails had proven unsatisfactory for use as the lines experienced increases in traffic, heavier freight and passenger loads, and larger locomotives. These changes led to the rapid wearing of the rail at the joints. The metal strips often pulled loose from the wooden stringers, sometimes curling back and ripping through the floors of passing cars, frightening if not injuring the occupants.[8]

In 1847 the New York legislature ordered all railroad companies within the state to re-lay their lines with solid iron rail:[9]

> Any railroad company whose track is now laid in whole or in
> part with flat bar rail on which steam power is used in pro-
> pelling cars, are hereby authorized to issue their capital stock
> or to borrow on the security of said road . . . an amount suffi-
> cient to enable such company to substitute upon their track or
> tracks the heavy iron rail, every lineal yard of which shall
> weigh at least fifty-six pounds, for the flat rail now in use. . . .
> And the neglect or refusal on the part of any such railroad com-
> pany so to substitute the heavy iron for the flat bar on their
> railroad track or tracks for the term of three years from and
> after the passage of this act shall be deemed a forfeiture of
> their charter.

In addition, the law provided specific financial penalties for
railroads which did not comply. A company was not permitted
to pay a dividend on capital stock of more than 3 per cent per
annum in 1847 if it did not begin reconstruction by January 1
of that year. Failure to complete the re-tracking by January 1,
1849, resulted in a ceiling of 1 per cent per annum on dividends until the work was finished. At a time when the dividends
of prosperous lines often reached 7 or 8 per cent per year, the
law offered a negative inducement to comply in order to attract
new and to retain old investors.[10]

The solid iron rail which came into general use during the
1840's was not a uniform product. There was a wide variety in
weight and patterns, with the pounds per linear yard increasing as the amount of traffic and the weight of the loads and
equipment mounted. Like the flat rail, the solid iron rail required supplementary products or supporting fixtures. At approximately three-foot intervals, iron chairs were used to brace
the rail and secure it to the wooden ties or sleepers. Iron spikes
were required to hold the rails and chairs in place. And, like

their predecessors, these items wore out, some from heavy use
and others because of their inferior quality. Iron rail that was
laid on many of the New York Central units between 1845 and
1849 had to be replaced in 1853.[11]

It was not until 1844, when the Mount Savage Iron Company
of Maryland rolled 500 tons of rail, that a domestic product
was available. Shortly after the Mount Savage works began
production, a number of other American mills rolled rail. The
output of American mills was never sufficient to meet demand
and large quantities of rail continued to be imported. When
world demand declined and prices fell in 1848–49, Americans
could no longer compete. Only two rolling mills produced rail
in 1850.[12]

Who furnished the iron for the construction of the New York
Central? Most of the rails used in the building of the original
roads came from Great Britain. Only a small percentage of
those laid down before 1853 were produced in the United
States. The principal suppliers—Dowlais, Cyfarthfa, Penydarren, Rhymney, Tredegar, Aberdare, and Nantyglo—were
all located in South Wales.

The Dowlais mills, in the nineteenth century, were among
the largest and most productive in the world. During the
1840's, when Sir John Josiah Guest was in charge of the
works, it operated eighteen blast furnaces, employed more
than 10,000 men, and was turning out more than 100,000 tons
of finished iron a year. Dowlais rails were generally held in
the highest esteem by American railroads, but Guest's policy
of refusing to exchange iron for railroad securities greatly
restricted their exports to the United States.[13]

The Cyfarthfa works were owned and managed by William

Crawshay, sometimes referred to as the "Welsh Iron King," and his brother, Robert. During the nineteenth century the mills grew enormously, and their rails were shipped in huge quantities all over the world. The Crawshays represented the prosperous era in Welsh iron making. They lived in medieval-styled castles, were despotic in their treatment of their employees, and were increasingly intolerant of any form of trade unionism.[14]

Very little is known about the operations of the iron works at Tredegar, Penydarren, or Rhymney, which were controlled by William Thompson and William H. Forman, London businessmen. But we do know that during the 1830s' they furnished a considerable number of iron rails used in the construction of the Camden & Amboy, the Baltimore & Ohio, the Philadelphia & Reading, and many other early railroad lines.[15]

The Aberdare and Nantyglo iron works belonged to Crawshay and Joseph Bailey, nephews of Richard Crawshay, the great ironmaster at Cyfarthfa. About 1810, Crawshay Bailey joined with his brother Joseph to work a share of some mines that had been left to him by his uncle. The business prospered and the Bailey brothers expanded their holdings by acquiring, in 1820, the Nantyglo and Aberdare properties and converting them into some of the finest iron works in the United Kingdom.[16]

The first purchases of British or Welsh rails for American railroads were made by company officials who visited Europe armed with maps, prospectuses, and letters of introduction from well-known American businessmen and government officials. They usually visited the iron works in South Wales and discussed the terms of prospective purchases with the iron-

masters at their company offices in London. After all, a face-
to-face discussion with the supplier seemed to be about the
best way to present one's case.[17]

During the 1840's and early 1850's British shipments of
railway iron to the United States had escalated to enormous
proportions. Ironmasters and iron merchants often found it
difficult to discriminate properly among the various groups of
officials and commission agents who descended on London to
market their securities or purchase rails and other supplies.
Consequently, many of them found it necessary to set up agencies in the United States to answer inquiries, investigate the
financial soundness of projected lines, and arrange for the
shipment and payment of any rails that might be ordered.

The problems associated with the international iron trade
during this period seemed almost endless. All rails were custom-made; purchases of ready-made rails were exceedingly
rare. Templates had to be drawn and the pattern sent to London for approval. The price of iron rails depended, of course,
upon the method of payment as well as the quality of the material used in the manufacturing. Rails purchased in return for
securities of the company obviously cost the most. The timing
of orders was very important. Large orders required several
ships. These had to be chartered months in advance, and if the
ironmaster failed, as he frequently did, to complete the order
on schedule, the financial loss could be substantial. Deliveries
were often delayed or cargoes lost because of unfavorable
weather. Moreover, shipowners had to operate on a schedule
of peak loads. The shipping season for the northern states was
very short, and cargoes arriving in New York after October
or November frequently had to be stored, at considerable ex-

pense, until the following spring. Nonetheless, by the 1840s' British shipments of railway iron had reached unprecedented levels.[18]

British ironmasters often chose as their agents in the United States established commission men, shippers, and iron merchants. Their business experience and contacts in the international trade made them ideal representatives. The New York firm of Richard and John Makin, a reputable commission merchant house with an excellent credit rating, represented the Dowlais Company for twenty years. It purchased materials in the United States that might be needed in the business and negotiated all contracts for iron with American railroads.[19]

William F. Weld was one of Boston's wealthiest and most gifted nineteenth-century businessmen. He sold hardware, served as a director of several railroads, imported railroad iron, and carried on an extensive commerce in his own ships with both the East and West Indies. At the height of his business career, Weld was probably the largest shipowner in the United States.[20] During the early 1840's Weld and his two partners, Richard Baker and William G. Weld, began the importation of iron rails and other railroad supplies as the American representatives of Thompson & Forman of London.[21] Weld supplied the iron for scores of American railroads, using the financial resources of his rich principals, his own money, and massive amounts of credits furnished by the Baring Brothers. The Barings took up Weld's account with a good deal of misgiving. They considered him "tricky," but his financial statements proved so satisfactory that, by the 1860s', Samuel G. Ward, the Barings' Boston agent, found no problem in extending the firm credit for as much as £100,000. "My reliance,"

he wrote, "is on their wealth, being out of debt, and their habit
of doing business correctly."[22]

About 1840, a group of Boston capitalists obtained a controlling interest in the lines west of Auburn through purchases
of forfeited stock, state-aid bonds, and other company security issues. William F. Weld, who represented the Yankee interest, was given a seat on the board of directors of the Auburn
& Rochester.[23] Thereafter, much of the iron purchased by these
roads passed through the agencies of Boston-based Wainwright
& Tappan or William F. Weld.[24]

Bailey Brothers was represented in the United States by
Wainwright & Tappan, Boorman & Johnston, Fullerton & Raymond, and Raymond & Fullerton. About 1840, two enterprising merchants, Henry C. Wainwright and Sewall Tappan,
founded a general mercantile and commission house in Boston.
They imported whiskey and ale from Scotland, bought cotton
for the textile mills of New England, and carried on an extensive trade, often in their own ships, in spices, tea, and coffee
with the Far East.[25] The transportation revolution of the 1830's
and 1840's brought the firm an increasing number of orders
for rails, spikes, and other supplies needed by the industry.
These were purchased on the basis of availability from a variety of manufacturers, but principally from the mills of Bailey
Brothers. The business prospered and within a few years Wainwright & Tappan devoted most of its time to the importation of
railroad iron.[26]

In 1813 James Boorman, who was born in England of Scots
ancestry, and John Johnston, another Scot, formed the mercantile agency of Boorman & Johnston. They imported Scot-
tish woolens, Madeira wine, and Swedish iron, and exported

large quantities of Virginia tobacco. For many years they held a monopoly of the Dundee–New York trade. Boorman also founded the New York Bank of Commerce and served for a time as president of the Hudson River Railroad. During the early 1840's the firm operated as independent commission merchants buying and selling iron on a consignment basis. But in 1846 it contracted with Bailey Brothers to serve as one of its agents in New York City for the sale of iron rails.[27]

Wainwright & Tappan and Boorman & Johnston reached an agreement in 1847 whereby Boorman & Johnston was to be Bailey's agent for New York and New Jersey, while Wainwright & Tappan had exclusive jurisdiction to the north and east of the Hudson River. The firms also agreed to share equally all the profits on contracts negotiated in the region south of New Jersey.[28]

There were some exceptions to this arrangement. Prior to 1847, Wainwright & Tappan had made contracts for iron with several western New York railroads. It asked to be allowed to complete these agreements, although the lines operated within the exclusive territory of Boorman & Johnston. It also requested permission to ship iron into the interior of the country via the port of New York during the navigation season, to take advantage of low freight rates. Under the terms of the agents' contracts, this business would ordinarily have belonged to Boorman & Johnston. The New York house agreed to the changes.[29] In 1850 the house of Raymond & Fullerton replaced Boorman & Johnston as Bailey Brothers' New York agent. Since Raymond & Fullerton also did business in Boston under the title of Fullerton & Raymond, Bailey Brothers named the firm its Boston agent.[30]

With three firms now representing Bailey Brothers in the United States, new contracts had to be drawn up for sharing the business. The parties announced that they would conduct their business affairs independent of each other but, in actual fact, they agreed to share the business and fix prices. In Boston Fullerton & Raymond channeled all Bailey Brothers contracts through Wainwright & Tappan, and at the end of each year they reported to each other on the amount of business negotiated during the previous twelve months and divided equally the 2 per cent commission paid them by Bailey Brothers. Since Wainwright & Tappan wished to retain its old western New York customers, all contracts relative to those companies that were signed before the agreement continued in force.[31] The arrangement enabled Wainwright & Tappan, which had highly profitable agreements at the time with the Auburn & Rochester for 4,600 tons, with the Tonawanda for 305 tons, and with the Attica & Buffalo for 3,250 tons, to fulfill its contracts without further controversy.[32]

The A. & G. Ralston Company of Philadelphia participated in the iron trade on both sides of the Atlantic. Alfred Ralston, the founder of the house, was a wealthy and generous Philadelphia merchant. He bought rails, spikes, lead, and small iron goods, often on a consignment basis, and assisted many early railroad companies, including the Mohawk & Hudson, with the importation of rails. By the 1840's Gerard and Robert R. Ralston, sons of the founder, became the principals of the house. Robert headed its Philadelphia branch and directed the American operations; Gerard resided in England where, in addition to being the trade consul for the American embassy he aided American agents in England to obtain railroad supplies.[33] When Erastus Corning visited London in 1840, it was Gerard who assisted him in the sale of his New York State securities.[34]

There were a great many independent commission men who imported iron on a small scale. One of them, Septimus Crookes of New York City, was described by his contemporaries as "highly respectable, of good character and habits and popular with the trade." Crookes furnished rails for the Schenectady & Troy in 1842 and the Utica & Schenectady in 1848 from the English mills of Abraham Darby in Coalbrookdale, Shropshire.[35]

One of the earliest railroad officials to travel to London to buy iron was Erastus Corning. He was born in Norwich, Connecticut, in 1794. At the age of thirteen he became a clerk in the Troy, New York, hardware firm of his uncle, Benjamin Smith, where he learned a great deal about the importation of small iron goods. He also became well acquainted with central and western New York, where most of the firm's customers resided. In 1824 he purchased the hardware business of John Spencer & Company in Albany, which he renamed E. Corning & Company.[36]

In 1825 Corning purchased the Eagle Air Furnace, an iron foundry and furnace in Albany. A year later he acquired the Albany Nail Factory in Troy. The factory was actually a small mill, capable of rolling approximately 800 tons of iron per year, about one-half of which was cut into nails. The mill served as the nucleus of Corning's iron manufacturing business, which became one of the largest iron and steel firms in the United States.[37]

Corning recognized early in his career that an important

relationship existed between the iron trade and the railroad industry. Company officials, he reasoned, had an unusual opportunity to make a great deal of money by negotiating contracts for supplying iron for the building of the road. In 1831 he purchased shares in the Mohawk & Hudson. He soon became a director and served for a time as its vice president.[38] In 1833 he was elected president of the Utica & Schenectady, a post he held until the line merged into the New York Central system.[39] During his long business career Corning acquired stock in virtually every road in central and western New York. He also made heavy purchases in the securities of a great many midwestern enterprises, such as the Michigan Central and the Hannibal & St. Joseph.[40]

Corning's career as an iron agent began in 1833 when he assisted the Mohawk & Hudson in obtaining 75 tons of iron through the agency of James Whitney in New York.[41] Four years later, Thomas Y. How, Jr., treasurer of the Auburn & Syracuse, solicited his advice on the use of lightweight rails for the company. Corning not only supplied the iron, but in doing so saved the railroad $15,000.[42] In the spring of 1838 Corning negotiated through Samuel Goddard of Birmingham, England, an order on behalf of the Auburn & Syracuse for 200 tons of rails and plate iron at $45 to $55 per ton. Goddard refused to name the manufacturer but assured Corning that it would come from "a most excellent House whose reputation stands high and upon whom we can place upmost [sic] dependence in regard to quality and adherence to specification."[43] Corning made payment for the iron in short-term notes through the London bank of Fletcher Alexander & Company.[44] By the close of 1838 Corning had arranged additional purchases for the Auburn & Syracuse amounting to approximately 600 tons.[45] He also acted, at times, as the purchasing agent for the Auburn & Rochester. In 1840 he arranged, on a commission basis, for the purchase of 1,400 tons of rails through the iron importing house of Davis Brooks in New York City.[46]

Late in November, 1840, Corning sailed for England. He carried with him $60,000 in New York State bonds that had been issued in aid of the Auburn & Rochester line, which he hoped to sell or exchange for railroad iron. He also wished to establish a working relationship with some London merchant bankers for the financing of future purchases of iron rails.[47] And, at the request of his partner, John Flack Winslow, he planned to seek information on British iron making processes that might be useful to their own firm.[48]

Prior to Corning's departure, Watts Sherman, the cashier of the Albany City Bank, approached Thomas Wren Ward, the American agent of the Baring Brothers, and urged him to extend Corning's credits so that he might make additional purchases of iron while in England.[49] But Ward declined. He did, however, write to William Goodhue & Company in New York to inquire about the condition of Corning's business affairs.[50] In reply, Goodhue stated that Corning enjoyed a good reputation, "was quite rich say $500,000," and that the house of Boorman & Johnston had extended Corning credits of $10,000 to $20,000. Goodhue added, however, that while his firm would extend Corning credits of $20,000, "in your case we would decline the application."[51]

On the basis of the information supplied by William Goodhue, Ward wrote the Barings that Corning's house, in all probability, would do well ". . . and in favorable times will come out rich," but "if (as I can well imagine may happen) there would be a great fall in landed property and an appreciation in the value of money, he would likely be in a difficulty. The Albany people are great speculators. I should not myself care to have the account."[52] But the Barings took a more optimistic view of Corning's future and agreed to extend him credits.[53]

While in England, Corning visited at length with a number of commission merchants, shippers, merchant bankers, and ironmasters. He saw a great deal of Goddard-Hill, Birmingham's leading commission merchants. He visited Cyfarthfa and discussed prospective purchases of rail for his New York lines with William Crawshay. The Welsh ironmaster claimed that his rails were "superior to any . . . ever sent to the United States," but he steadfastly refused to have "anything whatsoever to do with bonds or stocks of the U.S."[54]

Corning also called on A. & G. Ralston & Company. The Ralstons offered Corning rails to be manufactured by Thompson & Forman at a special price of £9 or $43.20 per ton, but refused to accept New York State bonds in payment. They did offer, however, to market the securities separately in London.[55] On January 26, 1841, Gerard Ralston reported that he had sold $40,000 of the state bonds at 85, or $34,000.[56] The balance of the issue hung on the market until April, when Ralston disposed of the lot at 81. The heavy discount represented a substantial loss to the railroad, but Ralston pointed out that he considered the price a fair one, since comparable bonds bearing interest at 5.5 per cent brought only 80 in New York. In the aggregate, Corning, during his stay in England, purchased and arranged for the shipment of more than 1,100 tons of railroad iron.[57]

After his return from London, Corning stepped up his activities as an iron agent. In 1843 he negotiated with the Rhymney Iron Company in South Wales for 1,611 rails for the Mohawk & Hudson.[58] The demand for iron increased substantially toward the end of the decade when the New York law required the re-laying of tracks with solid rails. In 1848 Corning purchased 3,500 tons of rails for the Syracuse & Utica, through Septimus Crookes, at $48.50 per ton.[59] American rails at the time averaged $71.00 per ton.[60] In the following year the directors of the Utica & Schenectady authorized their executive committee to purchase 6,000 tons of heavy iron rail in Great Britain.[61] Corning, a member of the committee, became the purchasing agent. Acting through John L. Clarke, his London agent, Corning contracted with the Dowlais works for 3,000 tons of iron rail at £5.10.0 or $26.50 per ton f.o.b. Liverpool.[62] The Baring Brothers arranged the financing.[63] Unfortunately, so many of the rails arrived in New York in such poor condition that Corning decided to purchase the balance of the order, 3,000 tons, from William Crawshay at Cyfarthfa for £5 or $24 per ton f.o.b. Liverpool.[64]

Corning's role as the major supplier for the lines in the western part of the state declined somewhat after 1850, when the financial control of those roads passed into the hands of Boston capitalists. After the Auburn & Syracuse and Auburn & Rochester consolidated in 1850, they built a second road parallel to the Erie Canal between Syracuse and Rochester. Nonetheless, the new company, under the presidency of Henry B. Gibson, retained Corning to negotiate for the purchase of 3,000 tons of rails. These were obtained from the Dowlais Company at $40 per ton. Corning's commission of 2 per cent amounted to about $2,400.[65] Corning also received, at this time, an order for 3,000 tons of iron from the Rochester & Lockport. Watts Sherman, who was vacationing in London, made the necessary financial arrangements with Sir John Guest at the Dowlais mills.[66]

Not all the iron for the construction of the New York Central came from abroad. A large amount of rails, chairs, spikes, nuts, and bolts was manufactured in the United States. Corning also enjoyed a substantial share of this business, both as a manufacturer and as a purchasing agent. Most of the iron spikes used in the building of the Utica & Schenectady and the Auburn & Syracuse came from the mills of Corning & Winslow in Troy, New York.[67] In 1845 he represented the Mohawk & Hudson in the purchase of iron castings from Barnum & Richards of Lime Rock, Connecticut.[68] Corning also purchased from Cooper-Hewitt, owners of the Trenton Iron Works of Trenton, New Jersey, 2,300 tons of solid iron rail for the re-laying of the tracks of the Syracuse & Utica.[69]

But Corning held no monopoly on the sale of iron to the Central lines. In September, 1841, the directors of the Utica & Schenectady instructed their superintendent, William Young, to solicit bids for the re-laying of the road with heavy iron rails for delivery in 1846.[70] A. & G. Ralston offered to furnish Welsh rails at $55 per ton for immediate delivery or at $50 at some future date.[71] The Mount Savage Iron Works of Maryland submitted a bid of $85 per ton cash.[72] The best offer came from Cooper-Hewitt, who proposed to supply the rails at $71.50 per ton, payable one-half in cash and one-half in the 6 per cent bonds of the Utica & Schenectady. This marked the first and perhaps only occasion when one of the units of the New York Central was involved in the direct exchange of iron rails for company securities.[73]

In 1848 the Utica & Schenectady reopened negotiations with Cooper-Hewitt for the purchase of 3,000 tons of heavy rail at $67.50 per ton and for 2,000 tons at $60 per ton, payable, as in the earlier contracts, one-half in cash and one-half in bonds. Dudley B. Fuller, Cooper-Hewitt's agent, explained the lower price by saying that the firm found it more economical to run the mills on a regular schedule with a large backlog of orders on which they made a fair profit than to operate them with only a few orders on which they made a high profit.[74]

After the formation of the New York Central system in 1853, the directors of the new company contracted for enormous quantities of railroad iron. Many of the rails of the original lines that were laid down during the late 1840's were badly worn and needed to be replaced. Moreover, the company planned to construct a second track between Albany and Buffalo, a distance of 300 miles, to accommodate the anticipated increases in both passenger and freight business. During the period August 1, 1853, through July 31, 1854, the company obtained through E. Corning & Company $1,098,407.30 worth of railroad iron.[75] To help finance these purchases, the Baring Brothers extended Corning credits amounting to approximately £100,000.[76]

In December, 1854, a group of stockholders, residing mainly in the Boston area, voiced concern over the practice employed by the company in the purchase of supplies. To them, the funneling of so many orders through Erastus Corning, the president of the New York Central, appeared to be a clear-cut case of conflict of interest.[77]

To resolve the issue, the board of directors appointed a committee composed of Charles Stebbins, a prominent Cazenovia attorney and former president of the Syracuse & Utica Direct and vice president of the Syracuse & Utica;[78] Joseph Battelle, an iron merchant and partner in the firm of Eggleston & Battelle;[79] and William H. Swift, a civil engineer and consultant on railroad affairs to the Baring Brothers.[80]

In its report, the committee cleared Corning of any wrongdoing. The prices paid to E. Corning & Company for goods and services, it was pointed out, were comparable to those charged by competing firms. The committee did recommend, however, that the New York Central avail itself more often of the services of iron company agents who negotiated contracts without commission. The stockholders' complaint had also alleged that the iron works of George H. Thatcher in Albany held a monopoly for supplying the Central with car wheels and that Corning furnished Thatcher with all the iron used in their manufacture. The committee reported that Thatcher's wheels were not the only ones used on the road, and that neither Corning nor any other Central employee held an interest in the firm.[81]

Despite the committee's recommendation that the Central should seek out additional suppliers, the company continued to award E. Corning & Company a major share of its contracts for rails and other railroad supplies. Between April 30, 1854, and September 30, 1866, the New York Central paid E. Corning & Company approximately $2 million for iron.[82]

Corning retired as president of the New York Central in 1864 and control of the road passed into the hands of the

Vanderbilt family. By the 1870's the American dependence on foreign iron and steel had lessened considerably, but both the Commodore and his son, William H. Vanderbilt, continued Corning's policy of buying the company's iron and especially steel rails from Great Britain, even though the cost was substantially higher than the home product.

TABLE I.

United States Mills: Initial Production of Iron Rails, 1844–1848[83]

Year	Firm	Location
1844	Mount Savage Iron Works	Mount Savage, Maryland
1845	Montour Iron Works	Danville, Pennsylvania
1845	Trenton Iron Company	Trenton, New Jersey
1846	Boston Iron Works	Boston, Massachusetts
1846	New England Iron Company	Providence, Rhode Island
1846	Phoenixville Iron Company	Phoenixville, Pennsylvania
1846	Great Western Iron Works	Brady's Bend, Pennsylvania
1846	Lackawanna Iron Works	Scranton, Pennsylvania
1847	Bay State Rolling Mill (Massachusetts Iron Co.)	Boston, Massachusetts
1848	Rough & Ready Rolling Mill	Danville, Pennsylvania
1848	Safe Harbor Iron Works	Safe Harbor, Pennsylvania
1848	Avalon Iron Works	near Baltimore, Maryland

TABLE II.
Iron Purchased by the New York Central System, 1830–1866[84]

Railroad	Date	Amount	Price	Maker	Agent
Mohawk & Hudson	27 Sept. 1830	400 tons		English	W. J. Braun
	7 Sept. 1833	75 tons		Thompson & Forman	A. & G. Ralston
	19 Oct. —				
	5 Dec. 1843	1611 rails	$ 40.40/ton*	Thompson & Forman	A. & G. Ralston
	11 June 1851	800 tons		Welsh	Winslow Lanier
Schenectady & Troy	26 Jan. 1842	Rail		Darby	Septimus Crookes
	12 July 1842	Spike	5⅝¢/lb.	E. Corning	
	4 Mar. 1842	70 tons		Henry Burden	
Utica & Schenectady	8 Aug. —			Darby	Septimus Crookes
	16 Nov. 1835	609 tons	$ 30.50/ton*	English	Samuel Hicks & Sons
	21 Nov. 1835	1,140 tons		English	J. H. Whitney (E. Corning)
	21 Dec. 1835	45 tons–spike		E. Corning	E. Corning
	13 Feb. —				
	15 Feb. 1836	16,044 bars	$ 27,300.64	English	Samuel Hicks & Sons
	25 Feb. —				
	30 April 1836	1,009 ton bar	$ 11,971.99	English	Samuel Hicks & Sons
	17 Jan. 1843	43 ton plate	$ 35.00/ton	Welsh	Boorman & Johnson
	20 Jan. 1847	6,600 tons	$ 40.00/ton	Welsh	Boorman & Johnson
	7 Jan. 1848	3,000 tons	$ 71.75/ton	Cooper-Hewitt	E. Corning
	17 May 1848	2,000 tons	$ 67.50/ton	Cooper-Hewitt	E. Corning
	22 Sept. 1848	3,000 tons	$ 60.00/ton	Cooper-Hewitt	E. Corning
	11 Nov. 1848	250 tons	$ 48.50/ton	Guest	E. Corning
	20 July 1849	3,000 tons	$ 50.00/ton	Darby	Septimus Crookes
	5 Oct. 1849	3,000 tons	$ 26.60/ton*	Guest	E. Corning
			$ 24.00/ton*	Crawshay	E. Corning

Iron Purchased by the New York Central System, 1830–1866 (Continued)

Railroad	Date	Amount	Price	Maker	Agent
Syracuse & Utica	16 Oct. 1846	2,300 tons	$ 71.75/ton	Cooper-Hewitt	E. Corning
	21 Sept. 1848	3,000–3,500 tons	$ 48.50/ton	Darby	Septimus Crookes
	13 Oct. 1848	3,000 tons	$ 48.50/ton	Guest	David Wetmore
	31 Oct. 1848	244 rails	$ 48.50/ton	Welsh	Cooper-Hewitt
	22 Sept. 1849	40 tons	$ 55.00/ton	Cooper-Hewitt	Cooper-Hewitt
	18 June 1852	20 tons	$ 55.00/ton	Cooper-Hewitt	Cooper-Hewitt
Auburn & Syracuse	7 Feb. 1837	Rail		English	E. Corning
	26 July 1838	200 tons		Welsh	E. Corning
	6 Jan. 1847	1,000 tons	$ 71.75/ton	Cooper-Hewitt	E. Corning
	3 Mar. 1847	2,000 tons	$ 71.75/ton	Cooper-Hewitt	
	7 Nov. 1849	13 rails	$ 50.00/ton	Bailey Bros.	Cooper-Hewitt
Auburn & Rochester	7 Jan. 1837	36 tons	$ 65.00/ton	English	E. Corning
	15 May 1840	600 tons		Welsh	E. Corning
	16 May 1840	100 tons–spike		E. Corning	E. Corning
	14 Nov. 1840 -	700 tons–rail		English	
	15 Jan. 1841	1,500 tons	$ 34.25/ton*	Thompson & Forman	E. Corning
	1 Aug. 1843	10 tons	$ 50.00/ton	Welsh	E. Corning
	25 Mar. —				
	6 April 1847	1,000 tons	$ 68.50/ton	Bailey Bros.	Wainwright & Tappan
	24 June 1847	600 tons	$ 65.00/ton	Bailey Bros.	Wainwright & Tappan
	14 July 1847	1,000 tons	$ 62.00/ton	Bailey Bros.	Wainwright & Tappan
	27 Nov. 1847	1,000 tons	$ 47.00/ton	Bailey Bros.	Wainwright & Tappan
	15 Dec. 1847	1,000 tons	$ 60.00/ton	Bailey Bros.	Wainwright & Tappan
Rochester & Syracuse	21 Nov. 1850	3,000 tons	$ 40.00/ton	Guest	E. Corning
Rochester & Lockport	20 Jan. 1851	3,000 tons	$ 50.00/ton	Guest	E. Corning
	6 Aug. 1853	1,000 tons		Thompson & Forman	W. F. Weld

Iron Purchased by the New York Central System, 1830–1866 (Continued)

Railroad	Date	Amount	Price	Maker	Agent
Tonawanda	14 July 1847	305 tons	$ 62.50/ton	Bailey Bros.	Wainwright & Tappan
Attica & Buffalo	13 July 1847	250 tons	$ 62.50/ton	Bailey Bros.	Wainwright & Tappan
	30 Oct. 1847	3,000 tons	$ 61.30/ton	Bailey Bros.	Wainwright & Tappan
New York Central	22 June — 18 Nov. 1853	2,620 tons		Welsh	E. Corning
	23 Feb. — 2 Dec. 1854	14,916 tons		Welsh	E. Corning
	30 April 1855 - 19 Jan. 1856		$588,744.31		E. Corning
	1 Oct. 1863 - 31 Sept. 1864		701,027.46		E. Corning
	1 Oct. 1864 - 31 Sept. 1865		$171,438,14		E. Corning
	1 Oct. 1865 - 31 Sept. 1866		$145,590.04		E. Corning

*f.o.b. Liverpool

1. James M. Swank, *History of the Manufacture of Iron In All Ages* (New York, 1892), 432, 434, 435.

2. Stephen Salsbury, *The State, the Investor, and the Railroad* (Cambridge, Mass., 1967), 109, 107.

3. F. W. Taussig, *The Tariff History of the United States* (New York, 1903), 52, 56.

4. Salsbury, 107, 108.

5. Frank W. Stevens, *The Beginnings of the New York Central Railroad* (New York, 1926), 39–55, 163, 164, 211. For a comprehensive study of early locomotives, see John H. White, Jr., *American Locomotives: An Engineering History* (Baltimore, 1968).

6. Stevens, 163, 164, 211.

7. Stevens, 32–34; Minutes of the Board of Directors, Utica & Schenectady Railroad, Sept. 25, 1844, Records of the New York Central Railroad, Penn Center, Philadelphia. The collection includes minute books of the early units of the New York Central. The file of minute books is not complete.

8. Stevens, 36.

9. *N. Y. Laws*, Chap. 272 (May 12, 1847).

10. *Ibid.*

11. *Report of A Committee Appointed 4 January 1855 by the Directors of the New York Central Railroad Company at the Request of the Stockholders, authorizing certain examinations to be made of the "Acts and Doings of the Directors and Treasurer," subsequent to Consolidation 24 October 1855* (Boston, 1855), 13.

12. Swank, 434, 435.

13. *The Dictionary of Welsh Biography Down to 1940* (London, 1959), 321, 322.

14. *Dictionary of Welsh Biography*, 86, 87; *Crawshay Papers*, National Library of Wales, Aberystwyth.

15. Margaret S. Taylor, "The Penydarren Ironworks, 1784–1859," *Glamorgan Historian*, III (1966), 75–87; Invoice Books, XXII, 1836–42, *Rhymney Iron Company Papers*, Glamorgan County Record Office, Cardiff Wales.

16. *Dictionary of Welsh Biography*, 20, 21.

17. Thomas Wren Ward to Baring Brothers, Nov. 16, 1840, Baring

Papers, National Archives, Ottawa, Canada; William Crawshay
to Goddard-Hill, Jan. 5, 1841, Corning Papers, Albany Institute
of History and Art. The Corning collection consists of over
40,000 pieces of correspondence, largely incoming letters, concerned with Corning's long and varied business career.

18. George Wright (Liverpool) to Corning (London), Jan. 13, 1841,
Corning Papers; New York *Commercial Advertiser*, Dec. 18,
1832; Henry B. Gibson to Corning, Nov. 16, 1840, Wright to
Corning, Jan. 13, 1841, Corning Papers.

19. Ledger of the Mercantile Agency, New York, CCCXLVI, 630,
601a, 700, Dun & Bradstreet Inc. Records, Baker Library, Harvard Graduate School of Business. The collection consists of more
than 2,800 volumes containing credit reports on thousands of
businesses in the United States c. 1840–95.

20. Ledger of the Mercantile Agency, Suffolk County, Mass., LXVIII,
253, LXXXIII, 72, Dun & Bradstreet Records.

21. Wainwright & Tappan to Boorman & Johnston, Jan. 17, 1848,
Wainwright & Tappan Papers. The collection is primarily com-
prised of correspondence of the house, whose business was generally concerned with the importation of metal products and iron
rails. Baker Library, Harvard Graduate School of Business.

22. Samuel G. Ward to Baring Brothers, Dec. 20, 1862, Baring
Papers (Ottawa).

23. Auburn & Rochester Railroad Contracts, Mar. 25, Apr. 6, June
24, July 14, Nov. 27, Dec. 15, 1847, Contract Book, Wainwright
& Tappan Papers; Charles Seymour to John E. Thayer & Bro.,
July 15, 1850, Letterbook 1840–1851, Auburn & Rochester Railroad. Records of the New York Central & Hudson River Railroad
Company, Syracuse University. Virtually all of the business records of the New York Central system 1831–60 are in this collection, including stock and bond ledgers, transfer books, stock certificates, and limited correspondence of officers of the companies.

24. William F. Weld also sat on the board of directors of the Tonawanda Railroad, July 14, 1847 Contract Book, Wainwright &
Tappan Papers.

25. Ledger of the Mercantile Agency, Suffolk County, Mass., LXX,
601, 605, 611, Dun & Bradstreet Records.

26. *Ibid.*

27. Ledger of the Mercantile Agency, New York, CCCXVI, 74, 101a, CCCXL, 12, Dun & Bradstreet Records; New York *Times*, Jan. 26, 1866; New York *Journal of Commerce*, Jan. 26, 1866.
28. Wainwright & Tappan to Boorman & Johnston, Dec. 27, Dec. 30, 1847, Jan. 22, 1848, Wainwright & Tappan Papers.
29. *Ibid.*
30. Ledger of the Mercantile Agency, New York, CCCXVI, 151, Dun & Bradstreet Records; Wainwright & Tappan to Raymond & Fullerton, July 22, 1850, Raymond & Fullerton to Wainwright & Tappan, July 23, 1850, Wainwright & Tappan Papers.
31. Wainwright & Tappan to Raymond & Fullerton, July 22, 1850, Raymond & Fullerton to Wainwright & Tappan, July 23, 1850, Wainwright & Tappan Papers.
32. Tonawanda Railroad Contract, July 14, 1847, Auburn & Rochester Railroad Contracts, Mar. 25, 6 Apr. June 24, July 14, Nov. 27, Dec. 15, 1847, Contract Book, Wainwright & Tappan Papers.
33. Ledger of the Mercantile Agency, Philadelphia CXXXI, 262, CDXLVI, 564, 547, Dun & Bradstreet Records.
34. Corning (London) to A. & G. Ralston (London), Jan. 12, 1841, A & G. Ralston to Corning, Jan. 15, 1841, Corning Papers.
35. Ledger of the Mercantile Agency, New York, CCCLXXIV, 104, Dun & Bradstreet Records.
36. *Dictionary of American Biography*, IV, 446; Joel Munsell, *The Annals of Albany 1850–1859*, III, 295, 449; Albany *Argus*, Mar. 1, Mar. 15, 1825. For a detailed study of Corning's business career, see Irene D. Neu, *Erastus Corning, Merchant and Financier 1794–1872* (Ithaca, N.Y., 1960).
37. Thomas Turner to Corning, Apr. 5, 1834, Corning Papers; Ledger of the Mercantile Agency, Albany, N.Y., DXXXVIII, 82, 159, Dun & Bradstreet Records; Neu, 37, 60.
38. Neu, 61; Statement of Purchase, Oct. 27, 1831, Corning Papers; Alvin F. Harlow, *The Road of the Century: The Story of the New York Central* (New York, 1947), 19; Albany *Argus*, June 24, 1834.
39. *Dictionary of American Biography* IV, 446.
40. Neu, 85.
41. Ramsey Crooks to Corning, Sept. 7, 1833, Corning Papers.
42. Thomas Y. How, Jr. to Corning, Feb. 9, Feb. 17, 1837, How to

E. Johnson, Feb. 9, 1837, Auburn & Syracuse Railroad Treasurer's Book, New York Central Records (Syracuse).

43. Samuel A. Goddard (Birmingham, England) to Corning, June 29, 1838, Corning Papers.
44. Fletcher Alexander & Company (London) to Corning, June 19, July 3, 1838, Corning Papers.
45. How to Corning, Nov. 22, 1838, Corning Papers.
46. Henry B. Gibson to Corning, May 16, May 21, 1847, Corning Papers. Gibson was the president of the Auburn & Rochester Railroad.
47. William Crawshay to Goddard-Hill, Jan. 2, 1841, Corning to A. & G. Ralston, Jan. 12, 1841, Ralston to Corning, Jan. 26, 1841, Corning Papers.
48. John Flack Winslow to Corning, c. Nov., 1840, Corning Papers.
49. Thomas Wren Ward to Baring Brothers, Nov. 17, 1840, Baring Papers (Ottawa).
50. Thomas Wren Ward to Goodhue & Co., c. Nov. 17, 1840, Baring Papers (Ottawa).
51. Goodhue & Co. to Thomas Wren Ward, c. Nov. 17, 1840, Baring Papers (Ottawa).
52. Thomas Wren Ward to Baring Brothers, Nov. 17, 1840, Baring Papers (Ottawa).
53. Baring Brothers to Corning, Jan. 14, 1841, Corning Papers.
54. William Crawshay to Goddard-Hill, Jan. 2, Jan. 5, 1841, Corning Papers.
55. Corning to A. & G. Ralston (London), Jan. 12, 1841, Corning Papers.
56. Gerard Ralston to Corning, Jan. 26, 1841, Corning Papers.
57. Ralston to Corning, Apr. 17, Apr. 19, 1841, Corning Papers.
58. Rhymney Iron Journal, Oct. 19, 1843, Dec. 5, 1843, Rhymney Iron Company Papers.
59. Septimus Crookes to Corning, Sept. 21, 1848, Corning Papers.
60. American Railroad Journal, XXII, Feb. 3, 1849, 68.
61. Minutes of the Board of Directors, Utica & Schenectady Railroad, Jan. 9, 1849, New York Central Records (Philadelphia).
62. J. L. Clarke to Corning, June 12, 1849, Corning Papers.
63. J. L. Clarke to Joshua Bates, Oct. 23, 1849, Baring Papers (Ottawa).

64. Watts Sherman to Corning, Oct. 5, 1849, Corning Papers; Purnell to Wood, Oct. 18, Oct. 23, 1849, London House Letters, Dowlais Iron Company Papers, Glamorgan County Record Office, Cardiff, Wales.

65. Sherman to Corning, Nov. 29, 1850, Cammann & Whitehouse (New York) to Corning, Dec. 21, Dec. 28, 1850, Corning Papers.

66. Kitson to Wood, Jan. 20, May 3, July 1, July 5, 1851, London House Letters, Dowlais Iron Company Papers; Gilbert C. Davidson to Corning, July 17, Sept. 18, 1851. Corning Papers.

67. William Young to Corning, Dec. 21, 1835, Henry B. Gibson to Corning, May 16, 1840, Corning Papers.

68. Barnum & Richards to Corning, Jan. 14, 1845, Corning Papers.

69. Thomas Hewitt for Peter Cooper to Corning, Oct. 14, 1846, Peter Cooper Letterbook 1841–1845, Cooper-Hewitt Papers, Cooper Union, New York.

70. Minutes of the Board of Directors, Utica & Schenectady Railroad, Sept. 25, 1844, New York Central Records (Philadelphia).

71. A. & G. Ralston to Corning, Mar. 7, 1845, Corning Papers.

72. J. M. House to Corning, Mar. 20, 1846, Corning Papers. House was president of the Mount Savage Iron Works.

73. Cooper-Hewitt to Corning, Aug. 27, Oct. 10, Oct. 16, Nov. 4, Nov. 10, 1846, Corning Papers; Minutes of the Board of Directors, Utica & Schenectady Railroad, Nov. 24, Dec. 3, 1846, Jan. 20, 1847, New York Central Records (Philadelphia); H. H. Martin to Cooper-Hewitt, Dec. 4, Dec. 28, 1846, Letter book 1844–1849, Utica & Schenectady Railroad, New York Central Records (Syracuse).

74. Minutes of the Board of Directors, Utica & Schenectady Railroad, Jan. 25, May 25, 1848, New York Central Records (Philadelphia); D. B. Fuller to Corning, Jan. 29, 1848, Corning Papers. Fuller, of New York City, arranged contracts for Cooper-Hewitt.

75. *Report of A Committee Appointed 4 January 1855,* 13.

76. Samuel G. Ward to Baring Brothers, May 16, 1854, Baring Papers (Ottawa).

77. Albany *Evening Journal,* Dec. 13, 1854.

78. Ledger of the Mercantile Agency, New York, I, 258, Dun & Bradstreet Records.
79. Ledger of the Mercantile Agency, New York, CCCXVIa, 133, 200e, Dun & Bradstreet Records.
80. Salsbury, 269–73.
81. *Report of A Committee Appointed 4 January 1855*, 13.
82. Money Paid to Individuals, Iron Account with E. Corning & Co., Apr. 30, 1855–Sept. 30, 1866, Comptroller's Records, New York Central Records (Philadelphia).
83. Swank, 434, 435.
84. Information drawn from a variety of sources, including the New York Central Records in Syracuse and Philadelphia, the Corning Papers, the Cooper-Hewitt Papers at the New-York Historical Society and Cooper Union, the Wainwright & Tappan Papers, the Dowlais Iron Company Records, and the Rhymney Iron Company Records.

Anglo-American Investors and Investment in the New York Central Railroad

Harry H. Pierce

Europeans, particularly the British, Dutch, and Germans, have been investing in the United States since colonial times. Most of this investment has been portfolio in character and took the form of purchases of corporate or government securities rather than the direct construction and operation of industrial enterprises. Unlike their business stake in the Far East and Latin America, this export of capital was not accompanied by the emigration of thousands of workmen, engineers, financiers, and managers. By 1914 foreign investment in the United States amounting to nearly $5 billion was concentrated heavily in railroads.[1]

England during the nineteenth century had a large surplus of investment capital and a great many prosperous people who were anxious to speculate in the economic future of the New World. The Baltimore & Ohio, the Wilmington & Raleigh, the Camden & Amboy, the New York & Erie, and scores of other early American lines were financed at least in part from London. Prior to the Civil War, hundreds of company officials, promoters, and commission merchants shuttled back and forth across the Atlantic in search of money and materials for railroad construction.

Since all American railroads at this time were dependent upon Britain for their supply of rails, financial agents always tried to dispose of their company's securities on a contingent or "tied" investment basis. The ironmaster or merchant banker who took them often did so in return for a share in the road's lucrative iron business. In 1837 Moncure Robinson sold in London 20,000 shares of the common stock of the Philadelphia & Reading and nearly $400,000 of the bonds of the Richmond & Petersburg and the Richmond, Fredericksburg & Potomac because a substantial part of these funds was to be used for the purchase of railroad iron. The Illinois Central laid almost its entire track from Chicago to Cairo with Welsh rails paid for principally one-half in cash and one-half in construction bonds.[2] Occasionally, an ironmaster like William Crawshay or a merchant banker like George Peabody held on to his securities as an investment, but usually they were immediately resold through a broker or banker to the English public.[3] The customer ledgers of Heseltine & Powell and Foster & Brathwaite, London's leading nineteenth-century brokerage houses, are filled with the names of English investors who obtained their first American railroad securities in this fashion.[4]

What about iron for the New York Central? Perhaps 90 per cent of the rails used in the building of the original lines came from the mills of South Wales. Payment for this iron was always made in cash or in the company's short-term notes. Financial arrangements for these purchases were usually entrusted to company officials such as Erastus Corning, the president of the Utica & Schenectady (1833–53) and the first president of the New York Central (1853–64), or to Boston capitalist William F. Weld, a director of the Auburn & Rochester (1842–53). These men executed their orders using credits furnished them by the merchant banking house of Baring Brothers in London. Despite oft-repeated charges against him of conflict of interest for taking commissions on the sale of supplies to his own companies, Corning continued this unethical but lucrative practice long after the formation of the Central system.[5]

The financing of the original lines of the New York Central was unusual in the respect that none of the securities of these early companies were sold in England or on the Continent in exchange for rails, locomotives, or other supplies. The risk or venture capital raised for their construction was obtained almost entirely in New York or New England. Foreign capital did not move into the Central until after the consolidation of the roads in 1853.

When the securities of the New York Central reached the London market during the early 1850's, the ordinary Englishman who wished to invest in the road had only a superficial knowledge of the operation of the stock exchange and practically no experience trading in corporate issues. People of moderate means were virtually excluded at this time from participation in the management of British industry. The most important shipping companies, coal and iron mines, potteries, and textile mills were family-owned. Public companies were often little more than wealthy partnerships, and it was commonplace for them to issue stock with a nominal value of £50 or more. The Bank Act of 1844 set the par value of bank shares at £100—a price far beyond the reach of all save the very rich.[6]

Moreover, corporate securities were a relatively new phenomenon with no well-developed machinery for their distribution and sale to the public. The joint stock company as a device for mobilizing large amounts of capital had been successfully employed by enterprising merchants for centuries. But until its implementation or refinement by acts of Parliament in the 1850's and 1860's, which permitted any company to obtain a certificate of limited liability, the joint stock company was not a practical instrument for making the savings of middle class investors available for business undertakings. The English people were raised on the partnership rule of personal liability "to the last shilling and the last acre," and it was not until the last quarter of the nineteenth century that the concept of limited liability was fully appreciated and accepted.[7]

Most of the early holders of New York Central securities were successful merchants, bankers, brokers, and well-to-do civil servants. Nearly all were experienced railway investors or had close ties with the industry itself. John Ellis and Sir George Byng Paget, who were neighbors in Leicestershire, served as chairmen of the Midland Railway. William Moorsame was a distinguished engineer who executed the surveys for the Birmingham & Gloucester Railroad; his brother Constantine, also a New York Central stockholder, was chairman of the London & Northwestern.

From Parliament came Thomas Thomassen, the wealthy Manchester cotton spinner, and John Benjamin Smith, the chairman of Britain's Anti-Corn League. William Lassell was president of the Royal Astronomical Society, while Sir Charles Lyell achieved lasting fame as England's most distinguished geologist. The novelist William Makepeace Thackeray was a stockholder for only four years, but his friend Herbert Spencer, a former railroad engineer, editor of the London *Economist,* and authority on human evolution, held shares in the Central system for more than a quarter of a century.

England at this time also had a small but highly energetic group of Quaker businessmen. They played a prominent role both as promoters and investors in the development of English railways. The Society of Friends furnished much of the capital for the building of the Liverpool & Manchester, and one of their number, Edward Pease, "the father of English railways," was the president of the Stockton & Darlington. Unwilling to take the statutory oath required of judges and members of Parliament and barred by religious conviction from accepting titles or serving in the army or navy, the Quakers looked upon wealth rather than rank as a symbol of status.

Some Quaker families, such as the Lloyds, the Barclays, and the Gurneys in banking; the Cadburys and the Rowntrees in chocolate; the Ricketts in starch and bluing; and the Bradshaws in railway journals and timetables, attained considerable wealth and influence. Many Friends entrusted their surplus capital to the Quaker brokerage houses of Robert Benson and Foster & Braithwaite for investment in American railroads.[8]

One of the richest and most respected members of the Society was James Cropper, the founder of the great mercantile house of Cropper & Benson, commission merchants, shipowners, and speculators in grain and cotton. His firm developed a vast trade with the Far East and started the first line of packets that sailed between England and the United States. Cropper died in 1840, without, in all probability, risking a shilling personally in the United States, but much of his vast wealth was subsequently invested by his family in American rails. Two of his sons, John and Edward, invested heavily in more than thirty American railroads, including substantial long-run stakes in the New York Central.[9]

One of the most fascinating and affluent of all those who invested in the New York Central system was Benjamin Ingham, the English Croessus, who lived in Palermo, Sicily. Ingham was fortunate to have as his American broker and confidential financial advisor Schuyler Livingston, a close friend of Erastus Corning and the senior partner in the New York house of Barclay & Livingston. Livingston steered Ingham's millions into a score or more of profitable enterprises, many of which Corning pioneered or in which he held a substantial financial interest. There were no failures. Every investment just soared and returned a handsome profit.

Ingham began in 1847 with a small investment in the Mohawk & Hudson, but soon expanded his portfolio to include the shares of the Utica & Schenectady, the Mohawk Valley, the Syracuse & Utica, the Rochester & Syracuse, the Buffalo & Rochester, the Syracuse & Utica Direct, and the Rochester, Lockport & Niagara Falls. When these roads were consolidated in 1853 to form the New York Central, Ingham became the largest stockholder in the new company. Ingham died in 1861, leaving a fortune estimated at £9 million.[10] He may not have been the wealthiest man in the world, but he was certainly one of the largest and most successful investors of his day in American railroads.

Company officials ascribed the lack of any significant fresh British investment in the New York Central at this time to the absence of an office in London for the registration and transfer of the road's stock and to the unlisted character of its shares. A general agency, they reasoned, would not only facilitate the transfer of securities, but would serve as a clearing house for information about the company's affairs." Some brokerage houses such as Heseltine & Powell, responding to representations from their clients that American securities would be more attractive if some recognized market for them existed, began to make their own market for them. That is, they sold New York Central and other railroad stocks from their own supply. The price or book level was determined after correspondence with their agents in Philadelphia and New York.[12]

After some hesitation, the company asked its treasurer, John V. L. Pruyn, to proceed to London and establish the necessary facilities. Pruyn was hampered in his task by stories in the British press about the infamous Schuyler frauds involving the over-issue and sale of stock by the Harlem and the New York & New Haven railroads. In a series of letters to the London *Times*, Pruyn explained that such a calamity could not happen in his company. Unlike other railroad corporations in the United States, he argued, the Central employed not only a transfer agent but an independent bank, the United States Trust Company, which served as a registrar of its stock. Pruyn opened the agency in December, 1856; a week later, the company's shares were admitted to the London Exchange.[13] The operation of the agency was not an unqualified success. Some stockholders rushed to exchange their American for English certificates, but many preferred to continue the registration of their shares on the company's books at Albany, Boston, or New York in the hope (illegal, of course) of avoiding income taxes, stamp taxes, probate duties, or "just as a way of keeping their property out of sight."[14]

The bonded debt of the New York Central in 1861 amounted to $14 million. Approximately $9 million of this sum was issued in 1853 under the consolidation agreement in the form of debt certificates or 6 per cent premium bonds. These were issued to shareholders of the original lines and represented the estimated value of their stock above par. Since British shareholders in the company in 1853 were few and their holdings comparatively slight, only a very small amount of these securities was held abroad.[15] The New York Central also issued at this time $3 million in 7 per cent bonds that were convertible into stock at par. Samuel G. Ward, the Boston agent of the Baring Brothers, strongly recommended these securities to his principals. "All the sifting the railroads have undergone," he argued, "has not diminished the confidence of the public or of the holders in the safety of this road."[16] Nathaniel Thayer, the Boston financier and a director of the New York Central, offered to divide $2.5 million of the issue between the two houses. But the Barings refused. They disliked debenture bonds payable in dollars. They wanted mortgage bonds payable in sterling. The Barings did subsequently subscribe for $100,000 on their own account, but the balance of the issue hung over the market for two years until Duncan Sherman & Company arranged to dispose of them at par for a commission of 2.5 per cent and the right to buy $250,000 at 97½. Only about $400,000 was actually taken up in London.[17]

What happened to British investments in American railroads during the Civil War? Most sterling bondholders held on to their securities. But investors in currency bonds sold heavily, especially during the first two years of the conflict. Common stockholders were also net sellers, but the extent of their selling varied considerably from company to company.[18] The New York Central had no sterling issues outstanding at this time, and British investments in their dollar bonds were relatively insignificant. There were, however, 428 registered British stockholders owning 34,443 shares on September 30, 1861; four years later, there were 192 holding 19,779 shares.[19]

Why did the British sell or reduce their investments? It is difficult to generalize, but there was considerable sentiment in England during the Civil War against the North, particularly among the wealthy, aristocratic groups. Some of these may have sold their securities or at least refused to buy any more as a gesture of their anti-Union feeling. The British press, particularly the pro-Southern London *Times*, gave widespread coverage to the war, but investors in the New York Central and other Northern companies found little consolation in its columns. There was also a surprising number of influential Anglo-American merchant bankers on whom investors in the United States depended for advice and counsel who were sympathetic to the Confederate cause or lukewarm in their support of the Union. Quarrels among the partners at Brown Shipley & Company over the policy to be pursued toward the belligerents brought that firm to the brink of dissolution.[20] The Barings were subjected to repeated attacks in the press for their alleged Confederate sympathies. When Senator John Sher-

man, brother of General William T. Sherman, went to London
after the war, Samuel Ward suggested to the Barings that they
keep Russell Sturgis, a senior partner who had been outspoken
in behalf of the Confederacy, "out of sight during the Senator's visit."[21]

The public outcry, on both sides of the Atlantic, that followed the Trent Affair in December, 1861, undoubtedly led a
great many to believe that in the event of war between England
and the United States their investments would be confiscated.
Even such well-informed and experienced bankers as the
Barings became momentarily panic-stricken. "What policy,"
they demanded to know, "would the United States government
adopt toward the confiscation of private debts and stocks
standing in the names of foreigners if, unhappily, a war
should break out."[22] Secretary of the Treasury Salmon P.
Chase replied that "As there is no likelihood of a rupture
with England the question to which you invite my attention
loses most of its practical importance. . . . It is hardly assuming too much, however, to say that in no contingency will the
United States, when engaged in war with any recognized
power, forget the rights of private persons, subjects or citizens
of the hostile power or State."[23] The Barings were not completely reassured. They transferred some if not all of their
American railroad securities into the name of their agent
Samuel Ward in Boston or to the brokerage house of Ward
Campbell in New York.[24]

But unquestionably the vast majority of those who sold or
reduced their holdings at this time did so because of the declining value of the dollar and the effect it had on remittances
from the United States. In the spring of 1863 William Craw-

shay, the Welsh ironmaster, angered by the sharp rise in the exchange rates, ordered his American attorney to sell his shares in the New York Central. He further resolved (a resolution he failed to keep) "never to embark again in an American Railway."[25] New York Central shareholders whose stock was registered in London at this time had an added incentive for selling. Trading in the road's securities on the London Exchange practically ceased during the war. In December, 1863, the company closed its London agency and the holders of London certificates had to choose between selling their shares or transferring them to registry in Albany or New York.[26] A great many chose to sell.

After the close of hostilities, the United States experienced an era of unprecedented business expansion. The boom was fueled by an estimated $2 billion in foreign capital that flowed into the country from Germany, Holland, France, and Britain. Professor Leland Jenks has estimated that, during the period 1866–73, about a half-billion of this amount was invested in railroads alone.[27] Samuel Ward urged the Barings to make the acquisition of railroad securities the cornerstone of their postwar investment policy; they were, he predicted, as "certain as that of shoes."[28]

To what extent did the New York Central participate in this enormous influx of foreign funds? With the exception of a single sterling issue for £2 million that was brought out in London by R. Raphael & Sons in 1873, only a very small amount of this capital inflow went into the Central. The New York Central was not well-known in London at this time. Its shares had been listed on the London Exchange since 1857 but, despite the company's enviable dividend record, they never enjoyed anything like the popularity of the stock of the profitable Illinois Central or even that of the highly speculative Erie, Philadelphia & Reading, or Atlantic & Great Western. British investors tended to shy away from the shares of those lines in which there was a substantial public interest or whose management was under the control of one man. In September, 1879, less than $3 million of the road's $89 million capital stock and only $12 million of its $40 million funded debt was held abroad.[29]

On November 26, 1879, William H. Vanderbilt, president of the New York Central & Hudson River Railroad and the owner of 38 per cent of its capital stock, sold to a syndicate of international bankers and business associates of Jay Gould 150,000 shares at $120 a share. He also granted them an option to purchase by January 10, 1880, an additional 100,000 shares at the same price. In a supplementary agreement Vanderbilt reserved the right to participate in the profits of the pool by placing with them on joint account an amount of stock not exceeding 100,000 shares. He further pledged that neither he nor any member of his family would sell additional stock before December 31, 1880, or until the syndicate completed its operations. And, probably at the insistence of the syndicate managers, Drexel Morgan & Company of New York and Junius S. Morgan of London, Vanderbilt named Cyrus W. Field, Solon J. Humphreys, and J. Pierpont Morgan to the road's board of directors.[30]

The transfer of 350,000 shares of stock with a market value of more than $40 million was labeled the largest single transaction in corporate history, and the announcement of Vanderbilt's proposal in the press generated enormous interest throughout the financial world as investors and spectators alike debated the effects that this massive turnover of securities would have not only on the future of the New York Central but on the operations of rival roads as well. Wall Street enjoyed its most exciting day since the failure of Jay Cooke & Company in 1873.

The Central had been almost the personal property of the Vanderbilt family for more than a decade. Their interest in the line dated back to Civil War days, when Cornelius Vanderbilt began buying up the shares at bargain prices. When the old Commodore died in January, 1877, he left nearly all his railroad investments to his son, William.[31] For nearly three years, William H. Vanderbilt kept this huge inheritance essentially undisturbed. In the meantime, he employed much of his available capital for the strengthening of his position in those lines that connected the Central with the Middle West. He bought heavily into the Lake Shore & Michigan Southern, purchased voting control of the Michigan Central and the Canada Southern, and maintained a strong equity position in the Cleveland, Columbus, Cincinnati & Indianapolis.

Despite the damaging effects of the Panic of 1873 and the ruinous rate wars with the Pennsylvania and the Baltimore & Ohio, the earnings of the Central during the first decade of its Vanderbilt operations (1870–79) were sufficient to enable the company to re-lay its entire track from New York to Buffalo with heavy steel rails, provide freight and passenger service at an acceptable level, and still show "a profit of $7,500,000 over and above the regular 8 per cent dividend paid out on the capital stock."[32] By the close of the seventies the financial outlook for the Central appeared unusually bright. The nation

had fully recovered from the depression, and there was little
if indeed any reason to suspect that Vanderbilt planned to sell
a single share of this property at any price and least of all to
a business rival as wily and unprincipled as Jay Gould.

It is not known for certain just when Vanderbilt decided to
sell his New York Central shares, but it was probably during
the summer or early fall of 1879. He could not have picked a
more propitious time. The fiscal year 1879–80 turned out to
be the most profitable in the company's history. Trunk-line
traffic rose sharply, and freight rates, despite competitive
flare-ups, remained relatively stable. Net earnings during this
period as well as profits per share soared to record highs.[33]

Late in October, 1879, rumors of an impending deal between Vanderbilt and the owners of the Wabash Railway cir-
culated in Wall Street, and stories detailing the progress of
the alleged negotiations appeared from time to time in the
financial columns of the newspapers.[34] A report by the prestigious New York Daily *Tribune* that Vanderbilt was about to
sell a controlling interest in the Central to Jay Gould was
ridiculed by the New York *World* as a "deliberate hoax" per-
petrated to depress the securities of the Erie so Gould could buy
them up later at bargain prices.[35] Cyrus Field, a director of the
Wabash and a close friend of Gould's, expressed great surprise that such a fabrication had been published and won-
dered why anybody would "swallow" it.[36] Vanderbilt himself,
in an interview with the New York *Evening Post*, insisted that
he had sold no stock, did not intend to sell any, and was not
discussing the matter with Gould or anyone else at that time.[37]

Meanwhile, J. S. Morgan, who was in New York at the time,
looking into the affairs of the Cairo & Vincennes railroad,

cabled his London office:[38]

Strictly confidential for your information only, negotiations pending some days in regard to buying William Vanderbilt's 12½ millions firm with option to buy 12½ New York Central Stock 120. After business nearly completed negotiations broken off owing to unwillingness fall in with our views in respect to balance Vanderbilt stocks. Negotiations may be renewed any moment. We can arrange satisfactory pay stated dates $ or 4% Funded, latter conditions will permit Syndicate utilize remainder Bonds, avoiding disturbances money market. Proposed purchases also had reference to friendly relations N.Y.C. & H.R., Lake Shore & Michigan Southern, Wabash RR's. Vanderbilt offers give Wabash R.R. interest 3 Directors Cyrus Field, Solon Humphreys, Ames. N.Y.C. & H.R.R. Simultaneously completion transaction Vanderbilt proposes reopen London Agency with J.S.M. & Co. for Transfer also payment dividend fixed exchange—Cable your views taking interest & amount in Syndicate if negotiations reopened.

The London office replied that it supported the plan wholeheartedly but was somewhat confused over the number of shares Vanderbilt planned to sell. "What amount will be issued," it inquired, "350,000 or 250,000."[39] Curiously enough, Vanderbilt did not own 350,000 shares at this time. He had to draw on his children's holdings to meet his commitments. Between November 29, 1879, and January 29, 1880, William H. Vanderbilt transferred to the members of the syndicate 298,500 shares; Frederick W., 15,000; Cornelius, 21,500; and William K., 15,000.[40]

Since the syndicate managers hoped to channel a substantial number of Vanderbilt's shares abroad, they attached great importance to the text of the prospectus that was being prepared for the London market.[41] William H. Burns, J. S. Morgan's son-in-law and partner, solicited the help of several well-known merchant bankers and brokers. He discussed the problem with James Capel, the investment counselors to Coutt's Bank, and with Charles Branch, a senior partner in Foster & Braithwaite, the large brokerage house with exceptional marketing strength among the English Quakers. He also consulted at great length with R. Raphael & Sons, the registered bankers and brokers who negotiated the Central's £2 million sterling loan of 1873 and who numbered among their customers many wealthy bondholders who might be interested in adding the company's common stock to their portfolios.[42]

One of the most difficult decisions that the syndicate had to make involved the inclusion in the prospectus of Vanderbilt's reason for selling his stock. Raphael contended that prospective British investors deserved an explanation. "Will Mr. Vanderbilt," he asked, "authorize the following":[43]

Shares now offered have been purchased from Vanderbilt, in whose family control, chief management, property have been vested many years. His object parting with a portion of stock may be found in great growth Company's business operation and capital, consequent necessity of sharing responsibility of management. By interesting gentlemen of large Railway influence experience in undertaking and by admitting their representatives to seats Board of Directors, he has established entire enterprise upon broader basis, and secured for his own line Traffic and western connections which might have been diverted to other Trunk lines. Vanderbilt retains presidency, present management Company, likewise large amount stock.

In a cable to its London partners, Drexel Morgan rejected the suggestion: "We decidedly do not think favorably of mixing Vanderbilt's name with the proposed issue, must stand upon property, its history, value, prospects which unquestionable."[44]

The price at which the stock should be issued also produced some disagreement. Drexel Morgan suggested $134 or $135 a share. Raphael wanted it to be "at least five per cent under the market giving the public a good turn. . . . An offering at $128 with four shillings and one and one half pence to the dollar," he argued, "might appear very attractive."[45] The syndicate committee fixed the price at $131.

At Vanderbilt's suggestion, J. S. Morgan devoted a great deal of time during his stay in New York to drawing up plans for the reopening of the Central's transfer office in London. Drexel Morgan considered the agency to be of little importance, but J. S. Morgan persisted.[46] The final draft of the prospectus provided for the opening of a full fiscal agency under the direction of J. S. Morgan, which would transfer stock free of expense to the shareholder and mail to each a check for dividends at the fixed rate of 49½ pence to the dollar.[47]

It is impossible to state on the basis of available information just how much each member of the syndicate realized from his speculation. The size and composition of the group as well as the amount of their holdings changed somewhat as Vanderbilt put more of his stock up for sale. The syndicate that took the first block of 250,000 shares from Vanderbilt was made up of the following:[48]

TABLE I

Name	Number of Shares
J. S. Morgan & Company	50,000
Jay Gould	20,000
Drexel Morgan	17,000
Drexel & Company	17,000
L. Von Hoffman & Company	15,000
Russell Sage	15,000
William L. Scott	15,000
John Newell	13,500
Winslow Lanier & Company	12,000
Morton Bliss & Company	10,000
Cyrus W. Field	10,000
Darius O. Mills	10,000
August Belmont & Company	6,000
Frederick L. Ames	5,000
Addison Cammack	5,000
Sidney Dillon	5,000
H. C. Fahnstock	5,000
Solon Humphreys	5,000
Edwin D. Morgan	5,000
Woerishoffer & Company	5,000
William L. Scott (for account of whom it may concern)	4,500

J. S. Morgan & Company originally subscribed for 50,000 shares. Of these, 2,500 were turned over to Edward H. Green, the husband of Hetty Green, and 2,500 were allotted to L. Von Hoffman & Company for its help in securing the "important cooperation" of R. Raphael & Sons in marketing the stock in England.[49] Morgan also arranged with several of his London friends to participate in the operation on a somewhat smaller scale:[50]

TABLE II

Name	Shares	Profit
Sir John Rose	300	$ 3,731.64
Seligman Brothers	2,000	24,887.65
George Hale Morgan	200	2,487.76
C. J. Hambro	1,000	12,438.83
Charles Branch	250	3,109.70
William Trotter	250	3,109.70
Frederick Rodewald	500	6,219.41

On June 9, 1880, Drexel Morgan, the syndicate managers, advised members that they had completed the accounts in connection with the sale of Vanderbilt's stock and that the "net profit per share, over and above the interest on the outlay amounted to $12.438826 per share." "We beg to state," they informed J. S. Morgan, "that your share on 41,300 shares amounts to $513,723.51 which we have credited to your special account." [51]

Morton Bliss & Company, an Anglo-American banking firm that specialized in government bonds and railroad securities, subscribed to 10,000 shares. But on December 6, 1879, George Bliss wrote to Levi P. Morton in London: [52]

> We have taken today through French, from J.D. Osborne 5000 New York Central under the recent arrangement . . . Perkins our next door neighbor, has repeatedly asked if we could not spare him some, and we now propose to do it, perhaps to the extent of two or three hundred shares. After this was done, French asked Mr. Bowdoin if we wanted 2500 shares more. . . . We feel like taking the stock & giving 2500 or 3000 to Morton Rose.

When the syndicate closed and the profits from the transactions were divided up, Morton Bliss received "a cheque for $186,000 odd of which 149 @ 150m$ sticks to us and $31,000 goes to London." On the basis of these figures, Morton Bliss held 12,000 shares and Morton Rose 2,500.[53]

Vanderbilt did not want Gould in the syndicate. But Gould was determined not to be left out.[54] He demanded full participation for himself and his friends as the price of his Wabash Railway business. When Vanderbilt refused, Gould threatened to turn away at Toledo his profitable eastbound traffic to the Baltimore & Ohio and build a road parallel to Vanderbilt's Lake Shore and Canada Southern lines between Toledo and Detroit. This maneuver would give Gould access to the city of Detroit and provide him with a through route by way of the Grand Trunk and the Great Western to Buffalo and the Atlantic seaboard at Portland, Maine.[55]

Unlike his father, William Vanderbilt was an appeaser, not a fighter. Despite his great wealth and powerful business position, he preferred negotiation and compromise to confrontation and conflict. Accordingly, Gould and several of his associates were made partners in the syndicate operation, and two of them, Solon J. Humphreys and Cyrus Field, were promised seats on the Central's board of directors. Gould in turn promised to continue the regular interchange of traffic between the Wabash and the Central and to abandon any plans for building a competing line between Toledo and Detroit.[56]

It should come as no surprise to learn that Gould did not honor his part of the agreement. Once the syndicate operation closed and the profits were divided up, he began the construction of a road linking Butler on the Wabash to Detroit, thus by-passing Vanderbilt's lines between Toledo and Detroit. Gould also made a twenty-year traffic contract with the Great Western which not only turned the business of the Wabash away from Vanderbilt's Lake Shore and Canada Southern roads but gave the Great Western access to Chicago over the Baltimore & Ohio, to the injury of Vanderbilt's Michigan Central.[57]

Of all the syndicate members none profited more from the sale of Vanderbilt's stock than Jay Gould. On his original subscription of 20,000 shares Gould was entitled to $12.43 per share or $248,600. During the latter part of January, 1880, despite favorable earnings reports put out by the company,[58] the shares of the Central fell on the Exchange, and Drexel Morgan had to enter the market to support the price. When this "manipulation"[59] of the securities failed to produce any significant improvement, some members of the syndicate became discouraged and urged that the unsold shares be divided up and the syndicate operation be brought to a close. But a majority supported a proposal to bargain with Jay Gould for "subsyndicating 50,000 shares with four months option for the balance."[60] Eventually, the syndicate managers and Gould reached an agreement whereby Gould took 67,700 shares that remained in the committee's hands, and his associates, Sidney Dillon, Louis Von Hoffman, Russell Sage, and several other international bankers, took the balance of approximately 40,000 shares. Or, as Brown Shipley so aptly phrased it, "the London Syndicate unloaded their Central Shares on Mr. Gould." Gould began selling his stock immediately. By the end of the year he held only 1,300 shares; six months later he had completely transferred out.[61]

Gould also profited substantially from his subsyndicate operation. No one can say precisely how much Gould made, but if he had sold his shares at the low for the day on which his stock was transferred he would have made $853,363; if

he had sold at the high for that day he would have received
$936,772. In any event, Gould's total profit from the sale of
Vanderbilt's securities must have exceeded $1 million.

The speed with which Gould disposed of his holdings and
his subsequent decision to build a line between Butler and
Detroit cast considerable doubt on the statement of Vanderbilt
and others that he had joined the syndicate primarily to
"harmonize" relations between the New York Central and the
Wabash.[62] A more plausible explanation, it seems, would be
that Gould joined the syndicate because it offered him an
excellent opportunity to make a great deal of money in a very
short time with a minimum amount of risk or effort.

Why did Vanderbilt sell his stock? It is difficult to attribute
his action to any single cause. According to Samuel Ward,
Vanderbilt was convinced that the burden of managing the
company was becoming too heavy to bear.[63] Vanderbilt probably suffered from arteriosclerosis and had been in ill health
for some time. It is just possible that he wanted to consolidate
his massive investments so they could be divided more easily
among his eight children in case of his death. Vanderbilt's
eagerness to take payment for his shares in government consols tends to support this argument. The bonds were abso-
lutely safe, yielded a good return, and enjoyed a high degree
of liquidity. The arrangement also enabled Vanderbilt to
avoid the risks of putting immense amounts of capital out of
reach for an indefinite period of time. He owned no 4 per cent
bonds in April, 1879; he held $47,050,000 in April, 1880.[64]
Approximately $42 million of this amount can be traced di-
rectly to his sale of New York Central stock. The balance may
have accrued from the sale at this time of nearly all of his

shares in the Michigan Central, the Canada Southern, the Lake Shore & Michigan Southern, and the Western Union.[65]

Vanderbilt claimed that in selling his shares he was moved by a double purpose of dividing with others the brunt of legislative attacks upon the Central and of giving to the public everything they could justly demand. In 1879 the New York legislature appointed a commission under the chairmanship of Alonzo B. Hepburn to investigate charges of monopoly and other forms of rate discrimination among the railroads in the state. Vanderbilt, who was closely interrogated by the committee's counsel, Simon Sterne, bitterly resented the inquiry:[66]

> There is today a great outcry against one man power. . . . This railroad committee means a railroad Commission to control the railroads of this State. . . . And with a Commission of politicians, what kind of a position would I be placed in, supposing I retained the controlling ownership of the New York Central? Why, either I must own the Commission or the Commission would own me. When such a thing impends, the best course a man can pursue is to withdraw, and go into something else.

Some historians have concluded from this statement that the Hepburn Committee so intimidated Vanderbilt that he sold his shares immediately to protect the company from hostile legislation. Perhaps this is so. Chronology alone makes the argument plausible. More probable, however, is that this was precisely the impression that Vanderbilt intended to convey.

By reducing his investment in the Central and by offering seats on the company's board of directors to such distinguished people as Cyrus Field, Solon J. Humphreys, and J. P. Morgan, Vanderbilt cleared himself of the charges of being a "monopolist" and of using his great power in a manner injurious to the public interest. It is difficult, however, to understand

how the public benefited by Vanderbilt owning fewer shares
and "Robber Barons" like Jay Gould and Russell Sage owning more.

Whatever reason Vanderbilt may have had for selling his
securities, surely the thought must have crossed his mind that
this was an unusual opportunity to dispose of, at a good profit,
a huge investment that had been locked up for a decade. The
syndicate's offer of $120 a share payable in cash or United
States bonds was a good one. With the exception of a single
transaction on October 16, 1879, when the shares sold for
$133, the all-time high for the stock was only 127. It is true
that the company had maintained an unbroken dividend record of $8 per share throughout the depression-ridden 1870's,
but the coverage was always very thin, and in at least two of
these years part of the dividend had to be paid out of capital.[67]
Furthermore, Vanderbilt was not an ordinary stockholder,
and any attempt on his part to realize in an open market on
such an enormous number of shares might have produced an
avalanche of selling and an immediate collapse in the value
of his holdings.

The vast market that J. S. Morgan anticipated for the New
York Central securities got off to a slow start. By March of
1880 fewer than 75,000 of Vanderbilt's shares had been sold
in London, and many of these were repatriated shortly after
the syndicate closed.[68] George Bliss wrote to his London partner, Pas de Grenfell, that "it looks as if your people were
going to return to us all the shares taken during the last
four or five months."[69] J. S. Morgan attributed the loss of
investor interest and the steady erosion in the price of the
Central's securities to Drexel Morgan's deal with Jay Gould

and the untimely dissolution of the syndicate. But the New York house emphatically disagreed:[70]

It is undoubtedly annoying that the stock with which both you and ourselves have been so conspicuously connected should have shared in the general decline which has lately taken place, but, on the other hand, we can not conceive how, even if the syndicate had not been dissolved, we could have prevented the occurrence. . . . There has been no misrepresentation and the property is more valuable today than when you first presented it to the English public. Whoever bought it when the issue took place have had the opportunity since to realize a fair profit and it seems to us that it would have been expecting entirely too much from our Associates to stand by the market and protect at their expense and at any cost this special Stock while the entire list was made the object of a well organized and powerful bear campaign simply because the English public speculative or otherwise, had become interested to the extent of 7 or 8% in this vast property.

Within a few months, however, the fortunes of the London agency took a turn for the better. J. S. Morgan made heroic efforts to bolster the slumping securities. He "talked up" the stock to his friends and bought heavily on his own account to arrest its decline on the Exchange. "We know confidentially," Brown Shipley informed its New York house, "that large orders went out to buy in your market yesterday—and this no doubt accounts for their coming $2 higher today. It remains to be seen whether sustaining the market is the way to succeed."[71] But the sale by Jay Gould and his friends of their interest in the road must have contributed enormously to the restoration of public confidence, especially in England. In September, 1880, there were 608 shareholders registered on the London books holding 122,558 shares; five years later there were 3,224 holding 246,401 shares.[72] Who purchased this stock? They were not, as it has been so often suggested, wealthy tycoons or titled aristocrats. They were just ordinary Englishmen who purchased the securities as a long-term investment. Many of these shares remained in family ownership until 1916, when the exigencies of the war forced them to sell to the British government.

TABLE III
New York Central Shares Held by the Vanderbilt Family

YEAR[1]	Comm. C.V.	W.H.V.	W.H.V. Executor	C.V.	F.W.V.	W.K.V.	W.H.V.'s daughters[2]	Vanderbilt Total	Total Shares
1863[3]	6,250	—	—	—	—	—	—	6,250	242,090
1870	55,530	50,000	—	20,000	—	20,000	—	145,530	448,158
1875	192,947	97,900	—	20,000	—	20,000	—	330,847	890,208
1876	203,067	97,900	—	20,000	—	20,000	—	340,967	896,087
1877	—	358,992	20,000	31,653	20,000	20,000	3,000	453,645	891,069
1878	—	354,210	20,000	31,653	20,000	20,000	7,500	453,363	891,846
1879	—	354,392	20,000	31,653	20,000	20,000	7,500	453,545	891,234
1880	—	83,292	—	9,053	2,000	7,000	7,500	108,845	891,109

[1] Books balanced as of September 30.
[2] William H. Vanderbilt's daughters were Emily Sloan, Florence Twombly, and Margaret Shepherd.
[3] Commodore Cornelius Vanderbilt first purchased New York Central stock on November 3, 1863.

Note: William H. Vanderbilt's sons were Cornelius, Frederick W., and William K. Vanderbilt.

TABLE IV

Share Ownership in the New York Central Railroad

YEAR [1]	Total Shares	Shares held in U.S.[2]	Number of Holders	Shares Held in England	Number of Holders
1853	230,856	222,320	2,831	8,536	45
1860*	240,000	207,828	3,898	32,172	354
1861*	240,000	205,557	3,821	34,443	428
1862*	240,000	209,624	3,321	30,376	375
1863*	242,090	219,643	2,681	22,477	286
1864*	243,860	224,579	3,001	19,281	197
1865*	245,910	226,131	2,931	19,779	192
1870	448,158	437,707	919	10,451	121
1875	890,208	852,357	3,907	37,851	308
1876	890,287	853,927	4,131	36,360	297
1877	891,069	858,119	4,267	32,950	302
1878	890,846	859,421	4,185	31,425	283
1879	891,234	862,197	4,271	29,037	262
1880	891,109	768,551	4,699	122,558**	608
1885	893,977	647,576	7,790	246,401**	3,224
1890	894,169	608,772	6,306	285,397**	4,202
1895	999,950	627,102	7,959	372,848**	4,594
1900	1,149,991	986,490	8,446	163,501**	2,105
1914	2,248,508	2,035,334	21,626	213,174**	3,132
1920	2,487,045	2,471,291	31,817	15,754**	254

[1] Books balanced as of September 30; however, in 1860–65 books balanced as of December 31 (*).
[2] Includes France, Holland, and Germany.
**London books only.

1. The estimate given here is based largely on my own research. Six months after the outbreak of World War I, Leonard F. Loree, the president of the Delaware & Hudson Company, reported that on the basis of returns from 105 railroad companies, foreigners held American railroad securities with a par value of $2,704,402,364.42. To this figure must be added all foreign holdings that were carried in the names of domestic bankers, brokers, or institutions and all investments in those bonds the interest on which was in default. A copy of Loree's report may be found in the library of the Association of American Railroads, Washington, D.C.

2. Minutes of the Board of Managers (1836–1837) of the Philadelphia & Reading Railroad, Records of the Reading Railroad Company, Terminal Building, Philadelphia; *The Fifth Annual Report of the Stockholders in the Richmond & Petersburg Railroad Company May 27, 1840* (Richmond, Va., 1840); *The Fourth Annual Meeting of the Stockholders of the Richmond, Fredricksburg & Potomac Railroad* (Richmond, Va., 1837), 42–44; Accounting Ledgers of the Illinois Central Railroad, New York Journals 1851–1856, Records of the Illinois Central Railroad, Newberry Library, Chicago.

3. Both Crawshay and Peabody invested heavily in American railroad securities. The financial records of George Peabody & Company are deposited in the archives of Morgan Grenfell & Co. Ltd., London, and in the Essex Institute, Salem, Mass. The Crawshay Papers are deposited in the National Library of Wales at Aberystwyth.

4. The customer ledgers of Heseltine & Powell are in the offices of the firm in Lawrence House, London. The records of Foster & Braithwaite are in Guild Hall Library, London.

5. I am indebted to Ann M. Scanlon, SUNY (Cortland) for this information about the activities of Corning and Weld as railroad officials and iron agents.

6. James B. Jeffreys, "The Denomination and Character of Shares 1855–1883," *Economic History Review*, XVI (1946), 45–55.

7. Herbert A. Shannon, "The Coming of General Limited Liability," *Economic History*, II (1931), 267–91.

8. Elizabeth Isichei, *Victorian Quakers* (Oxford, 1970), 182–86. Friends House Library in London has biographical information on thousands of English Quakers.

9. Frances A. Conybeare, *Dingle Bank: The Home of the Croppers* (Cambridge, 1925). James Cropper's sons John, James, and Edward were particularly active in the affairs of the Illinois Central, Michigan Central, and the Pennsylvania railroads. The financial records of James Cropper are in possession of the family at Tolson Hall, Kendall, England.

10. Raleigh Trevelyan, *Princes Under the Volcano* (London, 1972). The strategy of Ingham's investment policy can be traced in Schuyler Livingston's correspondence with Erastus Corning in the Corning Papers, Albany Institute of History and Art.

11. Minutes of the Board of Directors of the New York Central Railroad, July 17, 1853, Jan. 23, 1857, Records of the New York Central Railroad, Penn Center, Philadelphia.

12. P. G. Warren, *Heseltine, Powell & Co., One Hundred Years of Stockbroking 1851–1951* (London, 1951), 15.

13. John V. L. Pruyn to Erastus Corning, Nov. 28, Dec. 31, 1856, Corning Papers; London *Times*, Nov. 28, 1856; *Railway Times* (London), Nov. 29, 1856.

14. John V. L. Pruyn to Erastus Corning, Dec. 31, 1856, Corning Papers.

15. Henry V. Poor, *History of the Railroads and Canals of the United States of America* (New York, 1860), I, 272–74.

16. Samuel G. Ward to Baring Brothers, Oct. 3, 1854, Baring Papers, National Archives, Ottawa, Canada.

17. Samuel G. Ward to Baring Brothers, Nov. 10, 1854, Baring Papers (Ottawa); Duncan Sherman & Company to John V. L. Pruyn, July 23, 1856, Corning Papers.

18. *Railway News and Joint Stock Journal* (London), Feb. 20, 1869, 184.

19. See Table IV.

20. Aytoun Ellis, *Heir of Adventure: The Story of Brown Shipley & Company, Merchant Bankers* (London, 1960), 74–85.

21. Samuel G. Ward to William H. Seward, Feb. 9, Feb. 14, Apr. 17, 1867, Baring Papers (Ottawa).

22. Samuel G. Ward to Salmon P. Chase, Dec. 23, 1861, Baring

Papers (Ottawa).

23. Salmon P. Chase to Samuel G. Ward, Dec. 26, 1861, Baring Papers (Ottawa).

24. Samuel G. Ward to Baring Brothers, Dec. 31, 1861, Baring Papers (Ottawa).

25. William Crawshay to James Tinker, Mar. 20, 1863, Crawshay to Clarkson N. Potter, Mar. 23, 1863, Crawshay Papers.

26. The New York Central closed its Boston agency on May 1, 1865, and its Albany agency on July 31, 1868.

27. Joseph A. Schumpeter, *Business Cycles, A Theoretical, Historical and Statistical Analysis of the Capitalist Process* (New York, 1939), I, 335; Leland H. Jenks, "Railroads as an Economic Force," *Journal of Economic History*, IV, 9.

28. Samuel G. Ward to Baring Brothers, Sept. 5, 1864, Baring Papers (Ottawa). Ward recommended investment in railroads that were already in operation because they would be relatively free from competition for many years.

29. See Table IV; Ledger of Registered Stockholders, 1877–1882, Record of Registered Bonds Issued, 1873–1880, Records of the New York Central & Hudson River Railroad Company, Syracuse University. Commodore Vanderbilt negotiated in London with a dozen English banking houses before reaching an agreement with R. Raphael & Sons. He wanted to make the securities payable in dollars but the bankers refused. Brown Shipley & Company, who seriously considered taking the issue, reported that it was "quite impossible to make the investing public to whom the bulk of the Bonds must eventually go understand anything so intricate as that and we would have nothing to do with it." Letterbook, Brown Shipley to Brown Brothers, Jan. 14, 1873. The Brown Shipley Papers are in possession of their bank in London.

30. William H. Vanderbilt to Drexel Morgan & Company, Nov. 26, 1879. J. S. Morgan Papers, Morgan Grenfell & Co. Ltd., London. Shortly before negotiating the sale of his securities, Vanderbilt transferred "at arms length" 20,000 shares to twelve brokerage houses who held them until April 21, 1880, before transferring them back.

The New York Central Railroad became the New York Central

& Hudson River Railroad in 1870.

31. The will of Cornelius Vanderbilt was published in the New York *Times*, Jan. 9, 1877.

32. Edwin D. Worcester (treasurer of the New York Central & Hudson River Railroad) to J. S. Morgan, Dec. 1, 1879, J. S. Morgan Papers.

33. *The Forty-fourth Annual Report of the Board of Directors of the New York Central & Hudson River Railroad to the Stockholders for the Year Ending 31 December 1912* (New York, 1913), 97. This report contains a detailed summary of the financial operations of the railroad from 1870 to 1913.

34. New York *Evening Post*, Oct. 28, 1879. Gould owned, or at least controlled, the Wabash, St. Louis & Pacific Railway.

35. New York *Daily Tribune*, Nov. 21, 1879; New York *World*, Nov. 24, 1879.

36. New York *World*, Nov. 22, 1879.

37. New York *Evening Post*, Nov. 21, 1879.

38. Cable, Drexel Morgan to J. S. Morgan, Nov. 22, 1879, J. S. Morgan Papers.

39. Both the London and New York prospectuses refer to Vanderbilt selling only 250,000 shares. In a cablegram to his London office, J. S. Morgan explained the apparent discrepancy by saying, "We can issue only 250,000 as public know nothing about Vanderbilt's option." Cables, J. S. Morgan to Drexel Morgan, Nov. 23, 1879, Jan. 14, 1880, J. S. Morgan Papers.

40. Ledger of Registered Stockholders 1877–1882, Records of the New York Central (Syracuse).

41. Cable, Drexel Morgan to J. S. Morgan, Nov. 22, 1879, J. S. Morgan Papers; New York *Daily Tribune*, Jan. 6, 1880; New York *Evening Post*, Nov. 21, 1879; *Railway Gazette* (London), Dec. 5, 1879, 649.

42. Preliminary drafts of cables by William H. Burns (London) to J. S. Morgan (New York), *c.* Dec. 1879–Jan. 1880, J. S. Morgan Papers.

43. Draft of cable, William H. Burns to J. S. Morgan, *c.* Jan. 14, 1880, J. S. Morgan Papers.

44. Cable, Drexel Morgan to J. S. Morgan, Jan. 14, 1880, J. S.

Morgan Papers.
45. Draft of cable, William H. Burns to Drexel Morgan, *c.* Dec. 15, 1879, J. S. Morgan Papers.
46. Cable, Drexel Morgan to J. S. Morgan, Jan. 16, 1880, J. S. Morgan Papers.
47. Cable, Drexel Morgan to J. S. Morgan, Jan. 17, 1880, J. S. Morgan Papers. There is an original prospectus in the library of the London Stock Exchange.
48. William H. Vanderbilt to Drexel Morgan, Nov. 26, 1879, copy in J. S. Morgan Papers.
49. Cables, Drexel Morgan to J. S. Morgan, Dec. 2, 1879, Jan. 7, 1880, J. S. Morgan Papers.
50. Sundry Accounts Ledger No. 3, p. 94, J. S. Morgan Papers.
51. Cable, Drexel Morgan to J. S. Morgan, June 9, 1880, J. S. Morgan Papers.
52. George Bliss to Levi P. Morton, Dec. 6, 1879, Morton Bliss Papers, New-York Historical Society.
53. George Bliss to Levi P. Morton, June 10, 1880, Morton Bliss Papers.
54. *American Railroad Journal,* Nov. 28, 1879, 1317–18.
55. William H. Vanderbilt to Solon J. Humphreys, Nov. 10, 1880, copy in J. S. Morgan Papers.
56. Cable, Drexel Morgan to J. S. Morgan, Nov. 22, 1879, J. S. Morgan Papers.
57. William H. Vanderbilt to Solon J. Humphreys, Nov. 10, 1880, copy in J. S. Morgan Papers.
58. Cable, Drexel Morgan to J. S. Morgan, Feb. 2, 1880, J. S. Morgan Papers.
59. Cable, Drexel Morgan to J. S. Morgan, Feb. 11, 1880, J. S. Morgan Papers.
60. Cable, Drexel Morgan to J. S. Morgan, Feb. 2, 1880, J. S. Morgan Papers.
61. Letterbook, Brown Shipley to Brown Brothers, Apr. 29, 1880, Brown Shipley Papers; Ledger of Registered Stockholders 1877–1882, Records of the New York Central (Syracuse); New York *Daily Tribune,* Apr. 9, 1880.
62. William H. Vanderbilt to J. S. Morgan, Nov. 12, 1880, J. S.

Morgan Papers; New York *Evening Post,* Nov. 28, 1879.
63. Samuel G. Ward to Baring Brothers, Nov. 21, 1879, Baring Papers. These papers are in possession of the Baring Brothers & Company Ltd., London.
64. *Receipts for the Four Per Cent Consols of 1907, Individual Accounts Ledger 33,* p. 381, National Archives.
65. George Bliss to Levi P. Morton, May 7, 1880, Morton Bliss Papers. During the period 1878–80 Vanderbilt's holdings of Michigan Central shares declined from 54,000 to 2,000; Canada Southern from 60,00 to 2,000; Lake Shore from 115,500 to 71,000.

In 1879 the New York *Times* claimed that Vanderbilt "practically owns" Western Union (Nov. 29, 1879). In May, 1880, the *Chronicle* reported the sale by Vanderbilt to Jay Gould of 100,000 shares (*Commercial & Financial Chronicle,* XXX, 455). Vanderbilt's will makes no mention of owning any Western Union stock.
66. New York [State] Legislature, *Proceedings of the Special (Hepburn) Committee on Railroads, Appointed under a Resolution of the Assembly to Investigate Alleged Abuse in the Management of Railroads Chartered by the State of New York* (New York, 1879), III, 1205 ff.; New York *Evening Post,* Nov. 28, 1879.
67. *The Forty-fourth Annual Report of the Board of Directors of the New York Central & Hudson River Railroad to the Stockholders for the Year Ending 31 December 1912,* 97.
68. Minute Book of the Committee for General Purposes, XL, 281, Records of the London Stock Exchange, Guild Hall Library, London. On March 13, 1880, J. S. Morgan reported to the Committee that 74,054 of Vanderbilt's shares had been "unconditionally allotted." Of these, only 71,614 were actually sold in London. Drexel Morgan to J. S. Morgan, June 10, 1880, J. S. Morgan Papers.
69. George Bliss to Pas du Grenfell, May 20, 1880, Morton Bliss Papers.
70. Drexel Morgan to J. S. Morgan, May 18, 1880, J. S. Morgan Papers.
71. Letter Book, Brown Shipley to Brown Brothers, May 8, 1880, Brown Shipley Papers.
72. See Table IV.

The Business Elite of Antebellum New York City: Diversity, Continuity, Standing

Edward Pessen

The American economy grew at an amazingly rapid rate during the first half of the nineteenth century. Spurred on by its seemingly inexhaustible resources, a dramatically expanding population fed above all by great streams of Irish and German immigrants and the fecundity of its black population, and a transportation revolution that made of its continually expanding territories a *de facto* as well as a *de jure* customs union, the United States assumed a place in the world economy second only to that of Great Britain. Stimulated by European capital, which evidently found this nation's prospects as alluring as did the European peasants and working classes who flocked here, America's agricultural and industrial production soared and its shipping and commerce boomed in the years leading up to the Civil War.[1] Paralleling the dynamic expansion of the United States within the international community was the rise of New York City within the nation.

During the quarter-century following the completion of the Erie Canal, New York City became the nation's largest, its wealthiest, simply its leading city. By the 1850's its population of more than 600,000 almost equalled the total population of the three cities that came after: Philadelphia, Boston, and New Orleans. National leader too by a variety of other quantitative measures, whether for newspapers, schools, libraries, hospitals, churches, the institutions of the Protestant "benevolent empire," and reform organizations, as well as the principal art and "dramatic center of America,"[2] the great metropolis became the nation's financial and commercial capital. At midcentury the value of its exports and imports was greater than that of all other American ports combined. The business leaders—or what scholars of our time would call the economic elite—of nineteenth-century New York City were thus among the most influential capitalists in the western world. The purpose of this paper is to throw additional light on this important group of men.

Neither contemporaries nor later historians have ignored completely antebellum New York City's businessmen.[3] Yet inevitably the less than exhaustive literature has touched very lightly on certain of their activities and left unexplained several important questions relating to their role and their public behavior. In this paper I mean to glance briefly at and to portray in very broad strokes indeed a few of these neglected themes.

What was the economic character or nature of the great city's leading businessmen? If Walt W. Rostow's "take-off" thesis has application for Gotham as, according to him, it has for the American Northeast as a whole, then by the 1840's New York's entrepreneurs should have been heavily engaged in manufacturing and factory production.[4] While the paucity and impreciseness of the germane evidence has prevented re-

searchers in the past, as it no doubt will prevent them in the
future, from determining the proportions of their capital that
the city's men of affairs invested in this as against that form
of enterprise,[5] it does seem clear that relatively small portions
of the estates of the great wealthholders owed anything to
industrial investments.[6] And in that era, when great fortunes
were accumulated almost without exception in socially hon-
orific ways, the possessors of wealth were almost invariably
the very men and women who were their communities' business leaders.[7] According to the occupational designations offered by general and business directories published at the
time, fewer than 5 per cent of the city's wealthiest men and
women were "manufacturers," with many of these engaged
more heavily in the sale than in the production of commodi-
ties. While contemporary directories were hardly reliable
documents, in this instance they were not far wrong.[8]

More than forty years ago Robert G. Albion, the author of
what is still regarded as a classic study of New York port in
the mid-nineteenth century, concluded that the city's wealthy
businessmen were only slightly involved in banking and finance.[9] Albion was wrong. He was misled by the single designation—usually "merchant"—that the era's directories placed
alongside the names of most men of affairs and by the unreliable descriptions and classifications offered in the pages of the
Wealthy Citizens pamphlets that were published in the 1840's
and 1850's by the erratic Moses Beach.[10] The problem with
the directory attributions of a single occupation to most businessmen was its failure to communicate what was perhaps their
leading characteristic: the typical diversity of their economic
involvements. While very few of antebellum New York City's

successful men devoted themselves entirely to banking—or to any other single economic activity, for that matter—banking and finance were important in the affairs of most of them. Kenneth Porter was more accurate than was Albion when, writing a half-century ago of the sources of John Jacob Astor's great fortune, he concluded that although Astor "could not be classified as a banker . . . , like most moneyed men of his time . . . [he] was necessarily" interested in banking. Perhaps few leading New Yorkers were as heavily engaged in private banking as was Astor's contemporary, Isaac Bronson. Yet fewer still appear to have had no involvements of any sort either with banks or insurance companies.[11] Directorships on these corporations were a veritable catalogue of the city's wealthiest businessmen.

The antebellum business elite were usually classified as "merchants." The designation is a useful one, so long as it is construed as it was by men of affairs 125 years ago: a rubric that applied to persons with investments and even directorships and positions as officers of transportation companies, New York City lots and out-of-state real estate, mining, finance and insurance, manufacturing whether done in urban shops or in suburban factories, tanneries, and shipyards, among other things. As I have written elsewhere of Philip Hone, the onetime mayor of New York, social lion, community activist, *bon vivant*, and man beloved of social historians for the marvelous twenty-eight-volume diary he kept between 1826 and 1851, "in view of his more than a dozen simultaneous diverse business affiliations after his retirement from his family auction business—some in finance, some in transportation, some in manufacturing, some in mines, some in insurance, all in addition to his real estate investments—it is hard to say precisely what Philip Hone's chief occupation may have been."[12] Nor were Hone's numerous business interests unusual.

Those who define social class largely in terms of occupation tend to place successful merchants and members of the professions in different classes. One well-known problem with such classification is the internal differentiation within occupations.[13] The man who conducted a modest local retail storefront operation was no less a "merchant" than he whose vast shipping interests carried great quantities of goods to the distant corners of the earth; the lawyer who scratched out a living servicing the claims of the poor was no less an "attorney" than was a solicitor to the mighty. A less often noted weakness of this procedure is its separation of lawyers from businessmen, men who not only collaborated in business matters but who might be similarly successful members of the same family, treating them as though they belonged to dissimilar social categories. My point is that in antebellum New York, as in other cities, whatever might have been the differences in economic functions or even in income of leading lawyers and businessmen, they were equally members of their community's upper class, socially as well as economically.[14]

A swift answer, then, to the question that introduced this section, about the economic character of New York City's leading businessmen in the pre-Civil War era, is that they were men of diverse economic affairs. They were not the "industrial capitalists" of socialist legend. Such men there were—the Appletons and Lawrences of Boston, for example, or the Hendrickses of New York City—but they were rare. In that era the great wealthholders who made up the social and economic upper crust were "not so much the families which controlled the means of production as they were the families which controlled the vast wealth created largely through the exchange of goods produced."[15]

Such diverse individuals as the aristocratic French visitor Alexis de Tocqueville, Henry Clay, and the prominent New York City merchant William E. Dodge joined numerous other contemporaries in proclaiming that no job in antebellum America was more precarious than the successful business-man's. In an essay on "The Vicissitudes of Mercantile Life," Philip Hone's brother John observed that in contrast to "our worthy mechanics," who pursue "the even tenor of their way, the merchant is constantly exposed to all the chances of a most capricious life." It was, therefore, no wonder, he said, that an examination of the city's business directories over a five-year interval revealed that "an entire change of names takes place, and a generation passes off every five years."[16] Hone's ob-servation was based on something less than a detailed or pre-cise quantitative study, as was a similar statement made by Robert G. Albion a generation ago, to the effect that "mer-chants could not hope for the security which accompanied the more pedestrian occupations."[17] From the evidence that has been recently unearthed, Philip Hone appears to have spoken more truly than did his brother or Albion. Reflecting on the remarkable comeback he and many of his acquaintances made, a brief three weeks after the Wall Street fire of July 19, 1845, had apparently bankrupted and "ruined" them, Hone on Au-gust 12 wrote: "In no city of the globe does the recuperative principle exist in so great a degree as in our good city of

Gotham." In a paean to his class, he wrote of New York's merchants, "knock the stairs from under them, and they will make a ladder of the fragments and remount."[18]

Many small businessmen and marginal investors failed during the era, particularly after such debacles as the financial panics of 1837 and 1839 and the many fires that gutted Wall Street and other business districts during the period. In contrast, the several hundred wealthy and unusually successful families which occupied the city's highest social plateau were, like Philip Hone, able for the most part either to stand unshaken or quickly to recover from such crises. In doing so they no doubt benefited from gentle bankruptcy laws, mildly enforced, that enabled a "propertied bankrupt [to] conceal his assets and hire adroit lawyers to get him off scotfree on quibbling technicalities."[19] That the particular businesses or firms subscribed to by large wealthholders might go under did not mean the enduring failure too of the involved individuals. For as Philip Hone had observed, "throw down our merchants ever so flat, they roll over once and spring to their feet again."[20] Great wealth already in one's possession served as a marvelous cushion to financial shocks. The city's leading merchants of the 1840's were, with few exceptions, either themselves prospering in the 1820's or men born to families of wealth and privilege.[21]

Continuity among the city's business elite appears to have remained the rule during the 1850's and early 1860's. About 85 per cent of the city's 500 wealthiest individuals of the early Civil War era were members of families that had been among the wealthiest taxpayers of an earlier time. Nor does this mean that the 75 or so wealthy individuals of the later time who were missing from earlier lists of the rich were therefore poor boys and girls who had risen economically. It is quite possible that notwithstanding the absence of information on the wealth and social standing of their families, a number of them may have been descendants of well-to-do but out of New York State and New York City families. And the willingness of the city's tax assessors to accept without question the lies told them by wealthy property owners pleading poverty means that the absence of an individual from the tax lists—a happy lot that befell August Belmont, the House of Rothschild's agent in this country, and the prominent banker Preserved Fish, for example—is no certain sign of his earlier financial difficulties.[22]

Robert E. Gallman has recently engaged in a cliometric exercise designed to show that in the antebellum era wealthy Americans should constantly have been experiencing a substantial turnover in their ranks.[23] His argument is innocent of any detailed evidence on a single wealthy New Yorker. Such evidence, counterfactual statistical arguments to the contrary notwithstanding, discloses that the city's wealthy business leaders of the Buchanan-Lincoln era were with few exceptions of families that earlier had been successful. Life is not statistics. What cliometrics demonstrates *should* have been, was not in fact what *was*. Continuity, not discontinuity, was the rule among the metropolis's economic elite.

As for the imaginative notion put forth by John Hone and Robert G. Albion that the working people of antebellum New York City led economic lives more stable and secure than those of merchants, its accuracy would appear to depend on how one defines "stable and secure." While the necessary data bank remains less than full, much recent research indicates that the skilled artisans and journeymen who predominated in the working class of the era fared poorly. Whether security is defined in economic or emotional and psychological terms, men whose real income was low to start with and steadily declining, whose living standards were generally mean and marginal, who had no savings to fall back on when their precarious employment was either suspended—as it often was due to lack of supplies and indifferent managerial planning— or terminated, and the value of whose skill was constantly being eroded by their employers' increasing preference for poorly trained but cheap labor, would not in ordinary usage appear to have been enjoying secure lives.[24] The "shifting fortunes" attributed to merchants, on the other hand, concerned variations within what normally remained very much an upper class and most comfortable style of living. The fortunes of individual businessmen were distinct from and much more stable than the fortunes of the impersonal businesses that they invested in and controlled.

The final question to be considered in this paper concerns the place occupied by the business elite in the general affairs and life of the great city. The distribution of power and influence in antebellum New York City has recently been investigated, if less than exhaustively.[25] In this paper I do not mean merely to summarize the findings of earlier research but rather to put these findings in clearer perspective by relating them to our evidence on diversity and continuity among the city's business elite.

The standing of an individual or group can be measured in

a variety of ways, none of them altogether precise. No one can know, for example, what people of more than a century ago actually thought about the business community or how highly they regarded its leaders. Businessmen themselves and such contemporary publications as Hunt's *Merchants' Magazine* regularly propagated glowing accounts both of the achievements of mercantile leaders and of the popular respect such achievements ostensibly commanded. But it is impossible to enter into the minds of long dead and inarticulate men and women to ascertain their beliefs. It is easier and more sensible to infer the standing of businessmen by examining empirical evidence on their activities both within and without the business community.

As the holders of an inordinate share of the community's wealth, a portion that was not only great in relative terms but one substantial enough in absolute terms to enable them to enjoy a standard of living comparable to that of Europe's most sybaritic accumulators,[26] the mercantile rich enjoyed the admiration and envy that wealth everywhere evokes. If Tocqueville, Dickens, Mrs. Trollope, Michael Chevalier, Francis Grund, Harriet Martineau, and dozens of other mid-nineteenth century visitors—and natives such as Emerson and James Fenimore Cooper—can be believed, worship of the dollar and admiration of the men who made it were reigning beliefs in America, the closest thing to a secular religion.[27] As wealthholders par excellence, the metropolitan rich presumably basked in the glow created by their fellow citizens' adoration. Clearer than the esteem their wealth earned them are the influence and power their economic position made possible.

Brian Danforth has described in detail the "unrivalled"

control the merchant community exercised over New York City's financial institutions.[28] The banks they controlled in turn controlled credit through their discount committees determining who got how much and at what rates.[29] This came close to being a make-or-break power to aspirant entrepreneurs. As the owners of most of the city's real estate and as the capitalists who purchased the product turned out by artisans in the city's hundreds of shops and who hired the masters or foremen who ran these shops, the business elite controlled the land on which people lived and the jobs at which they worked. To paraphrase a catchy ad for a local rye bread, one need not be a Marxist to understand that economic power in general or power over property, banks, real estate, and industrial production in particular, is great power indeed. It is a very great power in its own right, quite apart from whether it *inevitably* gives to those who possess it the power over "superstructural" matters that economic determinists claim it does.

The fact is, whether inevitable or not, New York City's businessmen exercised much influence over significant other-than-economic institutions and areas of antebellum life. Local politics in New York, as in cities throughout the nation, was in the hands of successful businessmen and professionals, run by the propertied for the propertied.[30] Whether having to do with taxes and tax rates, local government spending, crime and police reform, street improvements, water supply and access to it, waste removal, or the other mundane but necessary matters that occupied mayors, councils, and boards of aldermen during the era, the policies followed by city government were usually policies in the interests of its business and propertied classes. In politics it is a fair assumption, I think, that governmental action—or inaction[31]—that appears to profit one group above all others reflects the power of the group in question.

This is not to say that businessmen were a selfish group concerned only with using government to promote their own narrow economic purposes. Businessmen were no more selfish than were other groups. My own impression is that they did *not* breathe hard on government in order to get things that they alone wanted. They did not have to. For whatever the reasons —and they are no doubt complex—government in mid-nineteenth-century New York City indeed behaved like a committee of the business class. And on the national level, the sensitivity shown by government toward the wishes and interests of the great cotton-producing section during the administrations of Pierce, Fillmore, and Buchanan was very much in accord with the wishes and interests of that substantial segment of the New York City merchant community that traded heavily with the South.[32]

New York City's businessmen, far from being preoccupied alone with business, politics, and self-interest narrowly construed, had time for many pursuits that are best described as public-spirited and high-minded. Despite the bad reputation for sordidness and selfishness heaped on them, particularly by partisans of Boston and Philadelphia, New York City's business elite were admirably active in a variety of voluntary associations devoted to one or another kind of uplift—religious and spiritual, cultural and intellectual, artistic, and social.[33] Their motives in undertaking such responsibilities were as complex as were their own personalities. Businessmen no more than other men lived by bread alone. If altruism, Christian zeal, and a sense of noblesse oblige urged them on, self-interest *broadly* construed was not altogether absent as a spur to their humanitarian activities.

At a time when laissez-faire and municipal parsimony were widely regarded as articles of faith, the great array of voluntary associations presided over by wealthy businessmen to deal with education, poverty, social welfare, and crime had an influence that matched if it did not surpass the power of government. Invariably the teachings that these organizations disseminated, along with their modest largesse, extolled businessmen and the prevailing social order in which they thrived. Those who propagated this ideology no doubt sincerely believed in it. The sour social theories of Thomas Skidmore, Frances Wright, Robert Dale Owen, George Henry Evans, and other contemporary nay-sayers were, I believe, literally unthinkable to men who had thrived under existing arrangements.[34] Far more convincing to them were the social doctrines of Malthusianism, which supplemented its pseudoscientific analysis of population-subsistence ratios with the advice that the poor were the authors of their own misery (and the rich of their own success). Pulpits, editors' offices, and orators' platforms in mid-nineteenth-century America—and in New York City—were for the most part occupied, if not by businessmen, then by men who preached this comforting social gospel and the variations on it that were so beloved of the economic elite of the day.[35]

None of this is to fault the era's business leaders. Most of them appear to have been sincerely religious and public-spirited men concerned with improving the community. In having achieved great wealth and economic power, maintain-

ing and enhancing the portion owned by their own families as
they shrugged off financial panics and natural disasters ruinous to lesser men, assuming great power over political and
other institutions, and in being blessed by the incessant propa-
gation of precisely those social ideas that justified if they did
not beatify them and their good fortune, the business leaders
had attained a success that epitomized the American Dream.
That all this did not necessarily make them the envy of their
time may have been due, ironically, to the very success of
their social indoctrination of the larger community. For did
it not teach that the mercantile life was frighteningly precarious, that wealth and great fortunes were here regularly
lost and wiped out, and that in this increasingly vulgar and
populistic democracy wealth and standing were at the mercy
of the masses and the political parties and social institutions
ostensibly dominated by the plebeian orders? The popularity
of the egalitarian myth attesting the weakness and subordi-
nation of the economic elite was, in view of the thin factual
basis and the downright inaccuracy of the myth, a striking
illustration of the actual power of those who most profited
from acceptance of and acquiescence in the myth.[36] Whether
this paradoxical state of affairs has changed very much in our
own time is an interesting question that awaits additional
research.

1. Douglas C. North, *The Economic Growth of the United States, 1790–1860* (New York, 1965); Stuart Bruchey, *The Roots of American Economic Growth, 1607–1861* (New York, 1965); Stanley Lebergott, *The American Economy: Income Wealth, and Want* (Princeton, N.J., 1976); Peter Temin, *The Jacksonian Economy* (New York, 1969); George R. Taylor, *The Transportation Revolution, 1815–1860* (New York, 1951); Walt W. Rostow, *The Stages of Economic Growth: A Non-Communist Manifesto* (Cambridge, Mass., 1960).
2. Alexander C. Flick, ed., *History of the State of New York* (New York, 1933–37), VI, 357–58, IX, 320; United States Census Office, *The Seventh Census* (Washington, D.C., 1853).
3. Freeman Hunt *Lives of American Merchants* (New York, 1857); Joseph Scoville ["Walter Barrett," pseud.], *The Old Merchants of New York* (New York, 1862–63); Stephen Girard, *The Merchants' Sketch Book and Guide to New York City* (New York, 1844); John W. Francis, *Old New York During the Last Half Century* (New York, 1857); William E. Dodge, *Old New York* (New York, 1880); Robert G. Albion, *The Rise of New York Port, 1815–1850* (New York, 1939); D. G. Brinton Thompson, *Ruggles of New York: A Life of Samuel B. Ruggles* (New York, 1946); Kenneth W. Porter, *John Jacob Astor, Business Man* (Cambridge, Mass., 1931); Richard Lowitt, *A Merchant Prince of the Nineteenth Century: William E. Dodge* (New York, 1954); Edward Pessen, *Riches, Class, and Power Before the Civil War* (Lexington, Mass., 1973); Brian J. Danforth, "The Influence of Socio-economic Factors on Political Behavior: A Quantitative Look at New York City Merchants, 1828–1844" (Ph.D. diss., New York University, 1974).
4. Rostow, *Stages of Economic Growth*, 38. For a sharp criticism of Rostow's thesis, see Robert William Fogel, *Railroads and American Growth: Essays in American Econometric History* (Baltimore, 1964).
5. For example, despite the enormous quantity of data Kenneth W. Porter was able to accumulate on John Jacob Astor's fortune and the investments responsible for it, Porter had no precise idea about either the dimensions of the fortune or the precise part played in creating it by Astor's diverse investments. Porter, *John*

Jacob Astor, passim.

6. I base this generalization on the private papers of dozens of New York City business leaders of the nineteenth century. For a detailed discussion of these sources, see Edward Pessen, "The Egalitarian Myth and the American Social Reality: Wealth, Mobility, and Equality in the 'Era of the Common Man,'" *American Historical Review*, 76 (October, 1971), 1031–34.

7. For the large degree of correspondence between New York City's wealthiest citizens of 1828 and 1845 and its merchants for the period 1828–44, compare Edward Pessen, "The Wealthiest New Yorkers of the Jacksonian Era: A New List," *New-York Historical Society Quarterly*, LIV (April, 1970), 145–72, with Danforth, "The Influence of Socioeconomic Factors on Political Behavior."

8. For an informed discussion of the weaknesses of directories, see Peter R. Knights, "City Directories as Aids to Ante-Bellum Urban Studies: A Research Note," *Historical Methods Newsletter*, II (September, 1969), 1–10.

9. Robert G. Albion, "Commercial Fortunes in New York: A Study in the History of the Port of New York About 1850," *New York History*, XVI (April, 1935), 159.

10. Never indicating the sources of the information that he claimed was given him by "insiders," Beach, the publisher of the notorious penny newspaper *The Sun*, put out a dozen editions of this strange publication. For a critical appraisal, see Edward Pessen, "Moses Beach Revisited: A Critical Examination of His *Wealthy Citizens* Pamphlets," *Journal of American History*, LVIII (September, 1971), 415–26. Albion also relied heavily on Scoville's *Old Merchants of New York*, which he praised for its "most useful material." For support of the view that "the character of [Scoville's] entertaining, gossipy work is not such as to entitle it to any weight," see the *New York Genealogical and Biographical Record*, 3 (1872), 180; 61 (1930), 342–43.

11. Porter, *John Jacob Astor*, II, 955–56; Grant Morison, "Isaac Bronson and the Search for System in American Capitalism, 1789–1838" (Ph.D. diss., City University of New York, 1973); James Sloane Gibbons, *The Banks of New York* (New York, 1858).

12. Pessen, *Riches, Class, and Power Before the Civil War*, 68–69.

13. Harold Hodges, *Social Stratification: Class in America* (Cambridge, Mass., 1969), 96; Leonard Riessman, *Class in American Society* (New York, 1959), 163–64; Paul Hatt, "Occupation and Social Stratification," *American Journal of Sociology,* 55 (1950), 533–47; Stephan Thernstrom, *The Other Bostonians: Poverty and Progress in the American Metropolis, 1880–1970* (Cambridge, Mass., 1973), 77.
14. Pessen, *Riches, Class, and Power Before the Civil War,* 165–299.
15. Edward Pessen, "The Social Configuration of the Antebellum City: An Historical and Theoretical Inquiry," *Journal of Urban History,* 2 (May, 1976), 279.
16. Cited in Girard's *Merchants' Sketch Book,* 43, 46–47.
17. Albion, "Commercial Fortunes in New York," 167–68. Albion's judgment appears to have been based only on a second-hand statement attributed to George Griswold and to quotations he drew from the unreliable accounts by Beach and Scoville. See note 10 above.
18. Manuscript diary of Philip Hone, vol. 23, p. 165.
19. Gustavus Myers, *History of the Great American Fortunes,* I, 72–73.
20. Hone, diary, vol. 23, p. 165.
21. Pessen, *Riches, Class, and Power Before the Civil War,* 85–87, 92–108.
22. My estimates of the proportion of later wealthholders who were well-to-do earlier is based on a comparison of the tax lists I assembled from the city assessors' notebooks for 1828 and 1845, William Boyd's listing for 1856–57, and *The Income Record, A List Giving the Taxable Income for the Year 1863, of the Residents of New York [City]* (New York, 1865). The latter document deals with income, which, while clearly related to wealth, is related by ratios likely to differ from one wealthy individual to another. On the reliability of *Boyd's New York City Tax-Book; Being a List of Persons, Corporations & Co-Partnerships, Resident and Non-Resident, Who Were Taxed According to the Assessors' Books, 1856 & '57* (New York, 1857), see Pessen, "The Wealthiest New Yorkers of the Jacksonian Era," 153, n. 12. My own lists for 1828 and 1845, as I explain in the latter essay, are based on the assessments on every item of New York City real property and

the assessed personal wealth of every individual in the city in 1828 and 1845.

23. Robert E. Gallman, "Professor Pessen on the 'Egalitarian Myth,'" *Social Science History*, 2 (Winter, 1978), 194, 199–203. For my refutation, see Edward Pessen, "On a Recent Cliometric Attempt to Resurrect the Myth of Antebellum Egalitarianism," *ibid.*, 3 (Winter, 1979).

24. For a discussion of the evidence underlying these generalizations, see Edward Pessen, "Builders of the Young Republic," in *The U.S. Department of Labor [Bicentennial] History of the American Worker*, Richard B. Morris, ed., (Washington, D.C., 1976), 56–80, 301–02.

25. Edward Pessen, "Who Has Power in the Democratic Capitalistic Community? Reflections on Antebellum New York City," *New York History*, LVIII (April, 1977), 129–55; M. J. Heale, "From City Fathers to Social Critics: Humanitarianism and Government in New York City, 1780–1860," *Journal of American History*, 63 (June, 1976), 21–46.

26. Pessen, "The Egalitarian Myth and the American Social Reality," 999–1004.

27. Edward Pessen, *Jacksonian America: Society, Personality, and Politics*, rev. ed. (Homewood, 1978), 24–26.

28. Danforth, "The Influence of Socioeconomic Factors on Political Behavior," 98–103.

29. Gibbons, *The Banks of New York*, offers an insider's invaluable report on how this was done.

30. See Pessen, "The Social Configuration of the Antebellum City," 294–96, for a discussion of political power in cities throughout the nation. For New York City, see Edward Pessen, "Who Governed the Nation's Cities in the 'Era of the Common Man?,'" *Political Science Quarterly*, 87 (December, 1972), 591–614; Pessen, "Who Has Power in the Democratic Capitalistic Community? Reflections on Antebellum New York City," 132–39.

31. On the importance of "nondecisions," see Peter S. Bachrach and Morton S. Baratz, "Two Faces of Power," *American Political Science Review*, 56 (December, 1962), 947–52; and Raymond E. Wolfinger, "Nondecisions and the Study of Local Politics," *ibid.*, 65 (December, 1971),1063–80.

32. Danforth, "The Influence of Socioeconomic Factors on Political Behavior;" Philip S. Foner, *Business and Slavery: The New York Merchants and the Irrepressible Conflict* (Chapel Hill, N.C., 1941).
33. Pessen, *Riches, Class, and Power Before the Civil War*, 251–80.
34. Edward Pessen, *Most Uncommon Jacksonians: The Radical Leaders of the Early Labor Movement* (Albany, N.Y., 1967).
35. Joseph Dorfman, *The Economic Mind in American Civilization* (New York, 1946), II; Clifford S. Griffin, *Their Brothers' Keepers: Moral Stewardship in the United States, 1800–1865* (New Brunswick, N.J., 1960) ; Charles C. Cole, *The Social Ideas of the Northern Evangelists, 1826–1860* (New York, 1954) ; Pessen, "Who Has Power in the Democratic Capitalistic Community?'„ 145–148.
36. On the egalitarian myth and its popularity, see Pessen, *Riches, Class, and Power Before the Civil War*, 1–4. The essential inaccuracy of the myth has been shown in dozens of modern works, which are discussed in Pessen, *Jacksonian America*, ch. 5.

American Business — Then and Now

Robert Lekachman

As a mere economist, I shall indulge myself in a practice
not in the best of historical taste: I shall shamelessly reflect
upon an aspect of the last century not (to the extent that this
is ever possible) in its own terms, but in the terms of today.
For this purpose, my nineteenth century commences in the
1850's and flickers out in the thunder and heat lightning of
the Great Crash of 1929.

In this era businessmen unquestionably dominated political
and economic life. As representative figures, they maintained
a firm grip on the popular imagination, sometimes as heroes
and role models, often as villains, but in either set of roles
as celebrities—human beings larger in scale than their fellows. Here, for example, is a comment by the London *Daily
News* on the occasion of Commodore Cornelius Vanderbilt's
1853 visit:

> America . . . is the great arena in which the individual energies
> of man, uncramped by oppressive social institutions, or absurd
> social traditions, have full play and arrive at gigantic devel-
> opment.
>
> It is the tendency of American institutions to foster the gen-
> eral welfare, and to permit the unchecked powers of the highly
> gifted to occupy a place in the general framework of society
> which they can obtain nowhere else. The great feature to be
> noted in America is that all its citizens have full permission to

run the race in which Mr. Vanderbilt has gained such immense
prizes. In other countries, on the contrary, they are trammelled
by a thousand restrictions. . . .[1]

One can tell the story (and many have) of the Du Ponts,
Morgans, Rockefellers, Guggenheims, and their few peers as
mostly a chronicle of exploited labor and of land and mineral
resources extracted by guile and corruption from the public
domain, the better to be ravaged and squandered for private
profit.

The muckrakers of the Progressive era—Ida Tarbell on
Standard Oil, Upton Sinclair on the meat trust (can any
reader of *The Jungle* forget how pure leaf lard was made?),
Thomas W. Lawson on *Frenzied Finance*, even Finley Peter
Dunne's Mr. Dooley—judged these magnates of industry and
finance as dangerous fauna. But the very titles of later volumes, such as Matthew Josephson's *The Robber Barons*, are
wry testimonials to the sheer scale of the stage upon which
these movers and shakers performed. A temperate biography
like David Hawke's *John D.*, an evaluation of the elder
John D. Rockefeller (based upon the nearly daily record
compiled by that meticulous soul and stored in the Rockefeller Archive Center) does leave one wondering how this
stuffy, self-righteous, pious, and utterly conventional family
man ever managed to organize a huge industry and to engage
in some of the practices he deemed essential to his objectives.[2]

For better or worse, these sponsors of their century, these
presiding geniuses of Daniel Boorstin's "consumption communities," these levelers of time and place, these coordina-
tors of continental markets, were go-getters, entrepreneurs of
imagination and guts, and always hustlers of the buck. In the

1920's good Americans didn't laugh when Calvin Coolidge identified the business of America as—what else?—business.

In his magisterial *The Visible Hand: the Managerial Revolution in American Business* (1977), Alfred Chandler pursued a theme similar to Boorstin's, though presented less colorfully. Chandler is a business historian in general sympathy with the institutions and individuals he has portrayed. All the more striking, accordingly, in his assertion (profoundly subversive to contemporary true believers in "free" markets even when they are invisible save to the eyes of faithful) that "modern business enterprise appeared for the first time in history when the volume of economic activities reached a level that made administrative coordination more efficient and more profitable than market coordination."[3] These words are a quiet and uninvidious but unmistakable way of stating that the modern corporation in its fully articulated form limits competition and substitutes planning of its operations and markets.

The achievements of older-style, individualistic captains of industry and finance were gained at a heavy cost to the health and well-being of employees, customers, suppliers, and rivals. Nineteenth-century industrialists suffered no agonies of conscience before arranging the calling out of the national guard or federal troops to break inconvenient strikes, hiring private armies of Pinkertons and thugs, spying upon and blacklisting union organizers and adherents, and jailing those who dared defy injunctions issued by complaisant judges, who were often in their previous careers legal counsel to large corporations. If the nineteenth-century magnate was a bore, boor, or both in private life, he was as a public figure dangerously arbitrary and casually heedless of the rights of others.

Early and late, there have been those who challenged the provenance of the century's economic achievements. Throughout his published work but most notably in *The Theory of Business Enterprise* (1904), Thorstein Veblen made a crucial distinction between business enterprise and the machine process. At least by the start of the twentieth century, the great fortunes of the *nouveaux riches* were the conseqence of financial manipulation, stock market rigging, conscientious sabotage (one of Veblen's better coinages) of the machine process, and artificially induced recession. Men who understood machines and scientific method kept the economy going. Men who shuffled paper and paper titles collected an increasing share of the proceeds.

In his ruminations about the future, Veblen's mood varied. When he felt cheerful, as in his late *The Engineers and the Price System* (1921), he forecasted the victory of engineers and technicians. The gloomier alternative, sketched in the concluding pages of *The Theory of Business Enterprise* and, fifteen years later, in *Imperial Germany and the Industrial Revolution*, envisaged the possibility of an alliance between businessmen and military leaders—votaries of archaic traditions of honor and glory.

Veblen did not have in mind the genuinely innovative organizational genius of a Ford or an Armour. He was pondering the maneuvers of the first J. Pierpont Morgan, who created out of nothing a huge fee for himself. Morgan paid himself $65 million or more for gluing together an assortment of independent steel companies and calling the new creation United States Steel. When he rested from his labor, presumably well content with his work, Morgan had added not a single ton of steel-fabricating capacity to the industry. Aside from further enriching himself, he had substantially diminished competition in a basic activity.

There is no need to labor further the point that large business has always been an object of suspicion to the public as well as to the social critics. Although the literature of exposé has run in cycles, nothing suggests a downward secular trend in its popularity. So to say subtracts nothing from the judgment that nineteenth-century businessmen exercised a dominion that their heirs, for the most part, can only envy and can only emulate in the meeker parts of this country and in momentarily hospitable, pro-capitalist portions of the Third World. With rare exceptions, nineteenth-century corporations controlled both Congress and the White House. Even when the accident of McKinley's assassination precipitated Mark Hanna's "damned cowboy" Theodore Roosevelt into the presidency, Roosevelt turned out to be more talk than action, at least as a trust-buster.

To inveigh after TR's fashion against the bad behavior of a few human beings is always a safe and entertaining diversion from structural difficulties too severe to be recognized. Later scholarship has even suggested that Taft had a better antitrust record than his predecessor and sometime sponsor. One is reminded of that amiable cynic Thurman Arnold's estimate of the Roosevelt performance: "Theodore Roosevelt, with his big stick that never hit anybody, accomplished two things. First, he convinced the public that if we would only drive politics out of the Department of Justice the laws were sufficient to make these big individuals really compete. Second,

he convinced corporate executives that it was a good thing to
hire public-relations counsel and show that they were follow-
ers of the true religion."[4] Was Arnold far wrong in describ-
ing antitrust as ". . . a ceremony which reconciled current
mental pictures of what men thought society ought to be with
reality. . . . In order to reconcile the ideal with the practical
necessity, it became necessary to develop a procedure which
constantly attacked bigness on rational legal and economic
grounds, and at the same time never really interfered with
combinations?"[5] For his pains, Theodore's cousin Franklin
appointed Arnold head of the antitrust division of the Department of Justice, a post in which Arnold did his ingenious best
to contradict his own derisive estimate of the Sherman Act
and its feeble progeny.

Nineteenth-century business leaders were powerful, self-
assured figures. But as an interest group, business was dominant mostly because other institutions were exceedingly weak
and their leaders figures of smaller scale than folk heroes or
folk villains like Andrew Carnegie, Henry Ford, Thomas Alva
Edison, J. P. Morgan, and John D. Rockefeller. It was embar-
rassing even to compare politicians like General Grant, Ruth-
erford Hayes, Benjamin Harrison, William Howard Taft,
even Teddy himself with titans who stood as tall in the land
as these paladins of pelf. In Horatio Alger's improving fables,
businessmen were role models, and lucky heroes married the
daughters of their bosses and lived happily ever after as
bosses in their own right.

The landscape was barren of opponents worthy of the corporate steel. Timid, conservative unions enrolled a small fraction of the labor force. The official leadership of the American

Federation of Labor[6] expressed its aspiration in the immortal response of Samuel Gompers to the query, What does labor want: "More." All during the gaudy decade of the 1920's, a period in which capitalists regularly advised the purchase of common stocks as the sure path to enrichment, unions steadily lost ground under the open shop assault of their employers. On the eve of the Great Depression, no more than three million Americans, concentrated in printing, construction, railroads, and the garment trades, owned union cards.

In the nineteenth as indeed still in the twentieth century, American politics has been persistently conservative. Even today, ours is the only major industrial society without a credible left. As MIT's Walter Burnham observed in the wake of the 1976 presidential election, the 50 per cent of the eligible electorate who did not bother to vote even for a President belonged for the most part to income and occupational groups whose members in western Europe usually support political parties of the left.

Signs of change are visible. For example, at the August, 1979, meeting in Chicago of the AFL-CIO Executive Council, that body tentatively and with qualifications actually contemplated the nationalization of major energy companies. Even more interesting has been the continued decline since 1929 of the prestige of corporate leaders. Consider as reasonably sensitive barometers of the public mood the August 6, 1979, issues of *Time* and *Newsweek*. The cover of the latter asked plaintively, "Where Have All the Heroes Gone?" Below this caption, Teddy Roosevelt yet again led the charge up San Juan Hill. Rummaging around for living heroes, *Newsweek* identified ten candidates, among them professional athletes Mu-

hammed Ali and Billie Jean King; reformers/activists Karen
Silkwood (recently deceased), Cesar Chavez, and A. Ernest
Fitzgerald (the Pentagon whistle-blower); law professor
Archibald Cox; and Betty Pollock, a Massachusetts foster
mother of eighteen. On the list was not a single businessman,
financier, corporate lawyer, Ford, Rockefeller, or Morgan.

As is its wont, *Time* approached the same theme more por-
tentously. Its editors "asked a variety of historians, writers,
businessmen and others in public life, 'What living American
leaders have been most effective in changing things for the
better?' " Using whatever undisclosed criteria emerged from
the nominating process, *Time* listed "50 Faces for America's
Future." They included some politicians, among them Marion
Barry, Carol Bellamy, Jane Byrne, David L. Boren, Gary Hart,
and Hamilton Jordan; several scientists; a conservative economist; Richard A. Viguerie, the titan of direct-mail fund
raising for conservative candidates; a college president or
two; and a miscellany of religious types, union leaders, and
public-interest activists. Women and blacks were prominently
featured, but not a solitary corporate leader made the grade,
unless one counts Brandon Stoddard, the American Broad-
casting Corporation vice president who in 1972 thrilled the
nation by the invention of the TV mini-series.

Here care is essential. One ought not leap happily or gloom-
ily to the conclusion that American business has lost power
and influence in our land. Such is hardly the case. As Charles
Lindblom persuasively argued in *Politics and Markets*
(1977), business continues to get its way most of the time on
issues of importance—taxes, trade policy, labor law—because businessmen not only compete in the normal political

market by subsidizing sympathetic politicians and periodicals, but they also always hold in their hand a trump card; the jobs and incomes which they provide. Corporations can and do desert communities politically unsympathetic and move to places where they are welcomed and subsidized.

For the time being, Lindblom appears to be right in implying that the declining popularity of business has not so far been associated with a parallel loss of power and influence. In the long run, however, it is hard to believe that the shifting reputation of business will be without political consequences. Let me postpone for a bit a speculation about these consequences and examine briefly the reasons for the declining legitimacy of the corporation and its managers.

The capitalism of the last century was indisputably a rough and even brutal set of arrangements, tough on factory workers, farmers, and small businessmen and unconcerned in general with losers. But, after its own fashion, it worked. As Marx and Engels pointed out in a famous passage of their *Communist Manifesto.*

> The bourgeosie, during its rule of scarce one hundred years, has created more massive and more colossal productive forces than have all preceding generations together. Subjection of nature's forces to man, machinery, application of chemistry to industry and agriculture, steam navigation, railways, electric telegraphs, clearing of whole continents for cultivation; canalisation of rivers, whole populations conjured out of the ground — what earlier century had even a presentiment that such productive forces slumbered in the lap of social labour?

In the century and a third that has elapsed since that reluctant salute, capitalism has split the atom, probed the mysteries of heredity, voyaged in space, transplanted hearts, sub-

stituted electronic images for print and computers and cal-
culators for arithmetic and grammar, transferred cooking,
baking, laundry, and sewing from homes to factories and
stores, and endowed average citizens of the richer lands with
opportunities for travel, recreation, and the manipulation of
mechanical toys confined in Marx's lifetime to the affluent if
available at any price.

In short, hotly pursuing profit, entrepreneurs have sponsored technical and organizational innovation and converted
the discoveries of basic science wherever possible into commercial opportunity. It states the obvious that until just yesterday—say October, 1973, when OPEC declared its em-
bargo—American capitalism commanded the allegiance or
acquiescence of most Americans because, despite glaring in-
equities, defects, caprices, and brutalities, it either delivered
the goods or credibly promised to deliver them in the near
The goods, above all, have included steady improvement in
future.
living standards, interrupted in recent experience only briefly
by recession. At 3 per cent average rates, per capita real
growth has translated into virtual guarantees of higher income
even for the occupationally immobile. An individual who
secured his first job on a factory assembly line, never won
promotion, and four decades later retired, could nevertheless
reasonably anticipate an enlargement of his real income of
no less than 150 per cent.

America also held out the prospect of social, financial, and
occupational mobility. Part myth, part fact, the national dream
of rags to riches has been fulfilled just often enough to reinforce the dominant national ideology of individualism and

equal opportunity. As parents aged and reconciled themselves to the disappointment of their own ambitions, they could take comfort from the hope that their children would fulfill the ungratified aspirations. Higher education has attracted its enormous constituency not out of affection for the liberal arts but in response to the conviction that appropriate credentials amount to lottery tickets in the drawing for the more lucrative prizes in the capitalist bazaar.

In its late, bureaucratic version (what tiny fraction of the public knows the names of more than a handful of the chief executive officers of the nation's hundred largest corporations?), capitalism's appeal is utterly material. So to say is to identify the fragility of a system devoid of romance and legend. For when economic growth slows and prospects of individual affluence and upward mobility falter and flag, former friends and beneficiaries hunt for alternate legitimations of their possessions, privileges, power, and wealth.

Growth has slowed. Worse, the chances of renewed acceleration are negligible. With desperate brevity, let me note some of the causes:

—As the supply of cheap fossil fuel diminishes, the era of abundant energy draws to a close.

—The presence and policies of OPEC have of course accelerated the chronology of this natural event.

—At best, a country as dependent as the United States is on imported petroleum must transfer a large and growing percentage of each year's increment to Gross National Product to foreign energy suppliers and soon perhaps to the owners of other scarce raw materials.

—Developed and developing societies are engaged in un-benign rivalry, under the auspices of multinational cor-porations. For workers in the advanced societies, this competition places steady pressure upon living standards and incorporates rising danger of job loss.

—Continuing shifts from commodity to service production at once reduce potential productivity gains and narrow access to entry-level jobs for new and sketchily prepared entrants to the labor force.

—As output is conventionally measured by the national income statisticians, growth is further reduced by the resources devoted to environmental preservation, worker health and safety, product reliability, and racial and sexual equality.

Just recently acquiring high visibility are the largest po-tential subtractions from statistically measured growth. These include:

—The enormous costs of rectifying the more malignant effects of corporate tendencies to use the natural envir-onment as a free dump and human beings as the targets of dubious or dangerous chemicals and preservatives. Hooker Chemicals is a conveniently egregious example of flagrant pollution. Cleansing soil and water supplies of poisonous wastes will require many billions of dollars of expenditure for years to come.

—More billions, by the handful, will be needed to main-tain, repair, and replace bridges, sewers, water mains, subways, and roads in the older cities of the Northeast and North Central states. A recent study by the Nova Institute estimated New York City's needs as $40 billion in the next decade merely to maintain, not improve, its capital infrastructure.

—I hesitate even to guess at the financial costs of treating and compensating the victims and their families of nuclear testing, carcinogenics, and dangerous industrial processes.

In sum, the overriding differences between our day and the last century is the contrast between the economic and politics of growth and those of distribution. The politics of growth has been comparatively benign. Its adepts can sidestep group and class conflict the better to concentrate upon the pleasanter problem of dividing up each year's increment to the Gross National Product. Hence no one ought be astonished that the virtual disappearance of the growth dividend has provoked numerous unresolved, inconclusive, and ill-tempered controversies over the incidence of taxes and distribution of federal grants in aid.

I yield to few in my low estimate of Jimmy Carter's presidential competence. But the most astute and magnetic of leaders would be having his troubles in these years, for nobody— not the actual unhappy White House occupant, not his few congressional allies, not his more numerous opponents—wants to play the new zero-sum game.

How will it all end? Prophecy is a mug's game. Let me engage in it all the same. For the moment, the national response is neurotic denial of reality—political paralysis, drift to the right, intractable inflation and as an unpleasant companion recession into the bargain. In due course all vacuums, the political variety included, are filled. At a guess, the residual strength of corporate influence, the weakness and division of the left, and the general conservatism of American political tradition and practice all combine to imply some drift toward corporatism, far less mitigated than now is the case by union, consumer, minority, and environmental countervailing pressures.

For the time being, the liveliest politics in the land is being played out inside the business community, which is split between Neanderthals like William Simon who are still thrilled by "Free Enterprise" and planning types like Felix Rohatyn, Henry Ford II, and David Rockefeller. In the end, sooner or later, the planners are likely to win. Unlike anachronistic free marketeers, the planners understand that in the grim context of slow or no growth, a new measure of coherence in national policy is the prerequisite to the social stability vital to their own interests. They are prepared to pay a price in welfare protection and social services, particularly if they can shift the tax burdens of providing them to Americans of moderate and middle income.

Corporatism is likely to be unstable and transitional. Resources will be too scarce to maintain or enlarge property incomes, preserve (let alone improve) average living standards, and finance even a frugal welfare state. As these realities sink into public consciousness, American politics is likely to polarize. On the left, if we are fortunate, will emerge strong sentiment for greater equity in the distribution of wealth and income and national planning focused upon social control of productive resources. On the right the danger is, as Robert Heilbroner among others has warned, of a shift to an outright authoritarian state.

Whatever happens, the day of the businessman as hero,

innovator, and proprietor of cornucopia is over. Like *Time* and *Newsweek*, I have my troubles locating substitutes.

1. Quoted in Sigmund Diamond, *The Reputation of the American Businessman* (Cambridge, Mass., 1955), 1.
2. David F. Hawke, *John D.: The Founding Father of the Rockefellers* (New York, 1980).
3. *Ibid.*, 8.
4. Thurman Arnold, *The Folklore of Capitalism* (New Haven, Conn., 1937), 217.
5. *Ibid.*, 207.
6. It says something about American labor that the AFL, for very nearly the first century of its existence, was led by only three men: Samuel Gompers, William Green, and George Meany. Gerontocrats are rarely radical.

Contributors

An Associate Professor of History at Hunter College of the City University of New York, DOLORES GREENBERG was appointed as the Director of Energy Policy Studies at that college.

She received a doctorate at Cornell University and has pursued an interest in late nineteenth-century American economic history since that time. Her book, *Financiers and Railroads 1869–1889: A Study of Morton Bliss & Company* has recently been published by the University of Delaware Press. Professor Greenberg is currently working on a study of financiers and American foreign policy in the late 19th century.

Distinguished Professor of Economics at Herbert H. Lehman College of the City University of New York, ROBERT LE-KACHMAN is noted as a governmental advisor, television personality, writer, teacher and lecturer. As a teacher he has been on the faculties of Barnard College, the State University of New York at Stony Brook and the City University of New York. Among his many publications are: *History of Economic Ideas; The Age of Keynes; National Income and Public Welfare; Economists at Bay; Inflation: The Permanent Problem of Boom & Bust.* His essays and reviews have appeared in leading newspapers and journals across the country.

Distinguished Professor of History at Baruch College and the Graduate Center of the City University of New York, Professor EDWARD PESSEN has made the merchant and business elites of the Jacksonian era his exclusive historical bailiwick.

A triple degree holder from Columbia University, he recently served as a Visiting Professor at the University of Toronto. No one studying the business communities in antebellum America is unfamiliar with his various contributions to that field of investigation. Among his many works are: *Jacksonian America: Society, Personality and Politics* (Dorsey Press); *Riches, Class and Power Before the Civil War* (D. C. Heath); *Most Uncommon Jacksonians* (State University of New York Press); plus multitudinous articles in the *American Historical Review,* the *Journal of American History, Political Science Quarterly,* and *The New-York Historical Society Quarterly.*

Author of the highly regarded study on governmental financial assistance to transportation facilities, *Railroads of New York: A Study of Government Aid 1826–1875,* published by Harvard University Press, HARRY H. PIERCE is currently Professor Emeritus of the Maxwell School of Citizenship and Public Affairs at Syracuse University. He devoted a lifetime professional career to teaching at Syracuse University and to research relating to the development of the American railroad industry.

GLENN PORTER holds the prestigious position of Director of the Regional Economic History Research Center of Eleutherian Mills-Hagley Foundation.

He possesses two graduate degrees in History from John Hopkins University. Dr. Porter is well known for his writings on various phases of American business and technological history. He is the author of *Merchants and Manufacturers: Studies in the Changing Structure of 19th Century Marketing* (John Hopkins University Press), *The Rise of Big Business, 1860–1910* (Crowell), and has contributed numerous articles to periodicals.

He has taught at the Harvard Graduate School of Business Administration and currently holds a concurrent professorial position at the University of Delaware.

A recent doctoral graduate of Syracuse University, ANN M. SCANLON is a Lecturer at the State University of New York at Cortland. Dr. Scanlon was a Ford Foundation Fellow, a Maxwell Graduate Fellow, a Syracuse University Graduate Fellow, and received a Newcomen Society of North America Award. Her essay on "Dun & Bradstreet's Credit Rating of Abraham Lincoln" appeared in the *Lincoln Herald* quarterly.

JOHN F. STOVER is Professor Emeritus of History at Purdue University. He obtained his doctorate from the University of Wisconsin and engaged in an extensive teaching career at Purdue. A specialist in transportation studies, Professor Stover has published *Railroads of the South, 1865–1900* (University of North Carolina Press); *American Railroads* (University of Chicago Press); *A History of American Rails, Turnpikes, Canals, and Steamboats* (Rand McNally); *The Life and Decline of the American Railroad* (Oxford University Press); and *Iron Road to the West* (Columbia University Press).

Editors

JOSEPH R. FRESE, S.J., is Emeritus Professor of History and the former Acting Dean of the Graduate School of Arts and Sciences, Fordham University. He has specialized in studies relating to the colonial and Revolutionary periods. His publications include "Early Parliamentary Legislation on Writs of Assistance" in *Publications of the Colonial Society of Massachusetts* and "Some Observations on the American Board of Customs Commissioners" in *Massachusetts Historical Society Proceedings*.

JACOB JUDD is Professor of History at Herbert H. Lehman College and the Graduate Center of the City University of New York. A specialist in colonial and regional history, he is currently editing *The Van Cortlandt Family Papers*. He co-edited *Aspects of Early New York Society and Politics*, and *The Loyalist Americans: A Focus on Greater New York*.

Index